John Du

The Mass

The Heart of Mission

EFFATA'  EDITRICE

Copyright © Effatà Editrice

ISBN 88-7402-001-5

Write to:

Effatà Editrice
Via Tre Denti, 1 – 10060 Cantalupa (Torino) – Italy
Tel. (+39) 0121. 35.34.52 – Fax (+39) 0121. 35.38.39
E-mail: info@effata.it
www.effata.it

First edition 2002
10 9 8 7 6 5 4 3 2 1 0

Cover photo: *Ikon of the Trinity* by Andrej Rublëv. A reproduction on sackcloth for the Major Seminary of the Consolata Missionaries (Addis Abeba, Ethiopia).

Translated from italian into english by Fr. Marco Bagnarol IMC, reviewed by James Tinkler and by Fr. Francis Dutto
Designed by Guido Pegone
Printed in Italy by Stargrafica – Grugliasco (Torino)

CONTENTS

Presentation .... pag.   5
Introduction... »   10

Christ is everybody's salvation .... »   12
Humanity has the mass! .... »   19
God gathers his people .... »   22
Run and clarify the world............................. »   27
The mass trasforms the world...................... »   36
One only body .... »   40
Consanguinity... »   45
God and man allied.................................... »   50
We become what we receive .... »   55
We are the body of Christ .... »   59
Mass becomes mission................................. »   62
Radiant with the Trinity .... »   68
A raised sign among the nations
    for the salvation of all .... »   73
The cure of the sun .... »   80
The eucharistic face of Mary .... »   86
A desire for the priesthood .... »   94
Missionary animation.................................. » 103
Sign of unity, bond of charity....................... » 108
Thanking .... » 113

CONTENTS

PRESENTATION

Eucharist and mission: two aspects appearing ever more frequently both in the Church's magisterium and in pastoral life. I had a clear confirmation of this when H.E. Mons. Renato Corti, upon concluding the National Missionary Convention of Bellaria, in order to rediscover the Church's missionary strength, asked those present to rededicate themselves to the Eucharist as their standard. *"We go to the Eucharist as disciples"* – he would say – *"but we come back from it as Apostles".*

This is an inner and pastoral experience possible for all, not only for the experts. All the more if it is true that participation in the Holy Mass remains the only experience of Christian community life in a position to resist the abandonment that the practice of faith undergoes. The celebration of the Eucharist on the Lord's day can really become the best place for missionary conversion, without adding anything else to the celebration itself. Everything in the Eucharist talks about universality. One only needs to live it out, and allow it to live, correctly.

The book that I have come to present is entirely aimed towards this goal. In order to affirm the unquestioned validity of its contents, I would like to recall two pastoral experiences that I have matured during my service as parish priest of the community of Sts. Michael, Paulinous and Alexander in Lucca's historical center.

The first refers itself to how I saw the essential reference to the centrality of the festive Eucharist grow within the community. A city parish, in fact, doesn't have many 'outer' elements that favour its union. That climate of geographical and human community so natural to a rural village and the inter-twining of relations and acquaintances that are fertile ground even to discover our own faith are lacking.

Those, instead, who desire life in the city due to the anonimity that characterizes it aren't few. From this point of view the small provincial town has nothing to be jealous of with regards to the big metropolis. Identical are the defects. Well then, exactly in that context, I was able to notice the degree to which the struggle to recognize ourselves as believers and as community of faith is sustained and nourished by the Eucharist. A considerable number of faithful has spiritually and affectionately deepened its own participation in the community by making reference to that specific festive eucharistic celebration where the most significant moments of its life would meet. The elderly, families, the youth and the young have thus learned to joyously recognize themselves as Jesus' disciples: table companions at the table of His Word and of His body and of His blood. Different events were occasionally organized to facilitate the involvement in an authentic participation and an ever greater number of people of different social classes and territorial origins.

It is in this context that I was able to rediscover – and in life this time, no longer in books! – that living in communion is already making the contents of mission actively present. Participating in the Eucharist with that intense adhesion that many ecclesiastical communities know how to express today, is finding once again the source and inspiration for one's capacity of giving witness with enthusiasm to the encounter with Jesus the Lord.

Here then is the second experience. The parish pastoral council, reflecting upon the orientations and the pastoral criteria of the community, holds the re-launching of a missionary commitment to be urgent. This choice was favoured in the light of the experience obtained when a priest, who had served the parish for some years, made himself available for missionary service in Brazil as a *'fidei donum'* priest. That choice hadn't remained fruitless for the community. Thanks to the awareness of the priest of the time, who would periodically go – even at length – to that mission, and to various lay people and families who would spiritually and materially accompany that experience, various suggestions returned from the mission so that the life of the parish might be renewed pastorally. From the initiative of the laity to the animation of the liturgies; from the evangelical reflection groups to some choices in the social field; from 'door to door' mission (evangelization of the territory) to 'side by side' mission (evangelization of people); and many other things as well.

I am sure that examples of this kind are numerous all around. It is the sign of how the universal mission has widely contributed towards renewing the most traditional pastoral work. In this sense the Pope's call at the Ecclesial Convention of Palermo – that the Italian Church not exhaust itself in conserving what already exists, but that it opens itself up with trust to pastoral conversion , finds its most fertile, receptive and determining ground exactly in its missionary commitment.

I therefore trust that this book, through the suggestive and rich indications that it offers by the hearts and pens of Fr. Giovanni Dutto will suggest to many readers an enthusing, eucharistic and missionary itinerary.

This is how the Pontifical Missionary Works has wanted to propose it: that the Mass be the heart of mission! And that ritual *'The Mass has ended, go in peace',* which concludes every celebration, be always and only the re-found beginning of how much being disciples has transformed us into apostles.

Mons. Giuseppe Andreozzi
National Director of the Pontifical Missionary Works

INTRODUCTION

These pages were born for a quarterly periodical that intends to squeeze the relatives and friends of a religious community into the spirit of the congregation. They are the young, the youth, the parents who generally benefit from the ordinary popular culture. They are 'dear' people, to whom true and vital things have to be transmitted, but in a familiar and simple style.

Experiences that have been lived, children and the poor from whom a lot can be learned constitute the sound track, that fascinates and facilitates, but which above all englobes sound doctrine and proposals of life in fullness.

Today, a *narrative theology* is talked about, which develops the literary genre of narration in harmony with Christian wisdom. There are even some novels with a theological background.

A spur to the revised re-edition of this work, which came out a few years ago, is the need to intrinsically rediscover the missionary dimension of the Eucharist. The doctorate of St. Teresa of the Child Jesus, the patroness of the missions, is recalling the Church with vigor to first of all live out contemplation in order to collaborate with Christ the missionary in the world's salvation. The spiritual sister of two frontier missionaries, she expresses her unity like this:

> *"You have united me forever*
> *to the works of a missionary*
> *with ties of prayer,*
> *of pain and of love.*
> *For him baptismal water*
> *will make of a one day old child*
> *the temple where God himself*
> *will live out of love".*

And from the National Convention celebrated in Bellaria (Italy), the Christian community is ruminating on the reason heard: *"The faithful enter the Mass as disciples; but they come out of Mass as Apostles".*

CHRIST IS EVERYBODY'S SALVATION

Dialogue makes things better understood.

I more clearly understood how Jesus is everybody's salvation by dialoguing with a Muslim friend.

The Christian era was just beginning where I had been sent as a missionary, in the desert of Marsabit in northern Kenya. For the first time the Church was peeping out in the midst of those semi-nomadic tribes.

The majority of people were animists: we would familiarly call them 'pagans'. But Islam had already arrived with merchants, who from Arabia or from Somalia would reach every little ethnic group, in order to sell some essential merchandise to it.

The new atmosphere of the Second Vatican Council was already being breathed in and *'dialogue'* was beginning to be talked about. I wanted to live out this new springtime climate with the Muslims and some of them sincerely became friends of mine.

One in particular. Where schools still didn't exist, he was called teacher *('mwalimu')*. He even did not know how to read or write, but he had the coveted task of looking after the Koran, the Muslim's sacred Book.

One day he came to me bringing the Book in a processional manner, with edifying veneration. It seemed as if the Book was trembling in his hands. I saw him coming and I thought to myself: *"These Muslims really have high regard for their Book!".* He respectfully bowed to me and remained looking at me at length. He then said: *"Father, my Book says that I'll go to paradise. And you, Father, where will you go?".* The Muslims believe that only they will save themselves; I, his friend, but not a Muslim, was at risk!

I had the Bible at hand.

I raised it up with new faith. Maybe even due to his example, my veneration for the Book of our salvation was very strong: it seemed to tremble in my hands and I thought to myself: *"This is the Book of all of humanity!".* I reassured my friend: *"My Book tells me that even I will go to paradise".* All of the great religions have sacred scriptures and the peoples of an oriental mentality in a particular way have great reverence for the sacred books. Mentioning the Book quickly cheered up my speaker. I then read to him St. Paul's talk on the history of salvation centered on Jesus who died and rose for us from the Acts of the Apostles. He listened with eagerness and found things never heard of before.

The Koran does not know anything about the story of Adam's fall and of the Redeemer's consequent promise. I continued: *"You see, due to Adam's and humanity's sin, an abyss has been dug between humanity and God. No man can save himself on his own. But God has created men in order to make them participants in his divine life. God wants all men to be saved. He has created us out of love. Therefore he has thrown a bridge over that abyss. Only one bridge. Therefore if you will be in paradise some day, it means that you have crossed over that bridge. And if I will be in paradise, it means that I too will have crossed over that only bridge".* My speaker looked at me serenely. I continued: *"Have you heard how my Book calls this sole bridge? It calls him JESUS CHRIST!".* We both had eyes shining with emotion. My friend bowed profoundly to me and slowly went away. I had told him about our faith.

In the Vatican II constitution 'Sacrosanctum Concilium', we read as in a catechesis: *"God, who wants all men to be saved and to reach the knowledge of the truth... sent his Son, the Word made flesh...*

Mediator between God and men. Therefore our perfect reconciliation with God came about in Christ. This work has been fulfilled in Christ the Lord, especially by means of the paschal mystery of his blessed passion, resurrection from the death and glorious ascension" (SC 5).

A little further it says that the Mass contains all of this history of salvation: *"Our Saviour during the Last Supper, on the night in which he was betrayed, instituted the eucharistic sacrifice of his body and of his blood, in order to perpetuate throughout the centuries, until his return, the sacrifice of the Cross, and in order to thus entrust to his beloved spouse, the Church, the memory of his death and of his resurrection"* (SC 47).

The following lesson to my Muslim friend would have been on the Eucharist.

I owe a great sense of gratitude to the Founder of the Missionary Institute of the Consolata Fathers, Brothers and Sisters, Blessed Joseph Allamano, because he founded his entire life upon this reality and he prepared me to particularly understand well the doctrine of Vatican II that the Eucharist is the *"Culmen et fons"* (height and source) of the whole of Christian life. He did it with his hammering: *"I want you to be eucharistic missionaries"*, and *"I*

15

want you to be sacramentines". But more than with words, he inculcated it into me with his life, splendidly centered around the eucharistic mystery, *"like a butterfly that flies around its flower without ever leaving it"*. His activities as a educator, administrator, director of various works, all had the same eucharistic flavour.

When he would go to sleep, he would accustom himself to center his last thought like this, as suggested by the Book of Esther: *"Tomorrow, I've been invited to dine with the king"*. And he would seem to have no other worry.

The morning bells would evoke the angelic trumpets for him, at the end of time, the day of the resurrection. It is a way in order to form oneself to the biblical mentality, the mentality of salvation history, as St. Paul teaches: *"We will all be transformed in an instant, in a blink of an eye, when the last sound of the trumpet will be heard. Because there will be a kind of trumpet sound, and the dead will rise in order to die no more and we will be transformed"* (1 Corinthians 15:51ff; 1 Thessalonians 4:16). Maybe he had read it in the Fathers of the Church: *"We observe the resurrection that will come about in the law of time. Day and night makes us see the resurrection. The night falls asleep, the day rises again"* (St. Clement I, letter to the Corinthians, 24).

On his morning alarm clock he had a very concrete and pleasant suggestion. Against every bad mood caused by the morning alarm clock, he had the habit, and he made a teaching out of it, of transforming it into Jesus' words to Zaccheus: *"Come down quickly, because today I want to stay at your home!"* (Luke 19:5). The 'hurry' is even the tone of enthusiasm and of energy that we have to impress upon our personality. But the motivation is really the magnetic pole which concentrates intelligence and will, for the whole day, in the great eucharistic event which on its own certainly gives colour and meaning to daily life.

Some phrases of his are full of light:

★ *"The Mass is the most beautiful time of our lives".*
★ *"You will always have the Eucharist in Africa: you will find your comfort in the missions' little chapels".*
★ *"The day should be a multiplying of aspirations which center themselves upon Jesus in the Blessed Sacrament. Every-thing is there: knowing how to practically live out of faith".*
★ *"The Mass sustains the world".*
★ *"A Mass would be enough in order to make whoever manages to celebrate it happy".*

I must even recognize that I find these things in all the saints. Every religious order can repeat them as their own. It's precisely because the eucharistic spirituality belongs to the Church.

The Mass is the heart of mission. When the world was dominated by evil and didn't have hope for salvation in itself, God made himself man and celebrated the paschal mystery, culminating on Calvary. Jesus incarnated himself, died, resurrected and ascended to heaven in order to restore humanity. Now, given that the Church of the Second Vatican Council has got us used to conceiving mission as God's salvific plan, we can make *'Mass'* and *'Mission'* coincide.

The real missionary is the Redeemer, and the Redeemer is here. The Church's mission therefore originates from the Mass, just like the mission of each and everyone of us has to depart.

Being 'eucharistic missionaries' is then so obvious. We can even simply say: 'eucharistic Christians', in order to indicate that the Eucharist is the fullness of life that is given to us in baptism, grows in the daily journey of faith and finds in it the height of every human expectation.

Christ made himself a bridge, so that the life of heaven floods the earth.

HUMANITY HAS THE MASS!

Marinette was a five year old French girl. An orphan, she lived together with two elder sisters, who were excellent educators. She felt a strong desire to receive Jesus and, when her sisters would approach to receive Communion, she would run after them and would say in a loud voice: "Me too!". She would be sent back every time with a candy and with the justification: *"You are too young"*. Marinette would cry.

St. Pius X would have given it to her. This Pope had in fact insisted on giving Communion to children as soon as they would have reached the use of reason, understood as the capacity to discern between the bread on the table and the one on the altar. *"We will have holy children!"*, he had said.

Marinette would have been passed with full marks by St. Pius X. But not by the French community of that time, which had established unbreakable criteria of age and of communitarian preparation.

It so happened one day that Marinette was being naughty at home. A sister of hers seized the occasion in order to give her a little lesson: *"Ah, the little saint, who wants to receive Communion and still doesn't know how to be on her best behaviour"*. Marinette yelled: *"But, it's exactly because I am not on my best behaviour that I have to run to Jesus: He will make me good"*.

If we substitute Marinette with all of humanity, we understand the history of salvation. Decadent man will never be able to save himself on his own. But *"God loved the world so much as to give his only begotten Son, so that whoever believes in Him will not die but have eternal life"* (John 3:16). And Jesus loved his own so much that *"He loved them right until the end"* (John 13:1) and wanted to give himself *"in order to gather the dispersed children of God in unity"* (John 11:52).

Ours is a history of sin, but it is not a history of depression and of desperation.

St. Bernard refutes Cain's discouragement: *"And therefore it is evident that he who said: Too great is my fault in order to obtain forgiveness* (Cfr. Genesis 4:13), *was mistaken. The fact is that he was not a member of*

20

Christ's community, nor could he get to know Christ's merits". The history of sin cannot therefore overcome the history of love.

And it is this history that we, instructed by St. Paul, call *"mystery"* or *"history of salvation"*. It is the design of God who from eternity loved us, created us and then redeemed us in order to communicate himself to us and to make us participants, in eternity, of his very same life. God *"loves first"* (1 John 4:19), beyond our understanding, and, as St. Thomas comments, we are the only people to have him so closely.

It is still St. Thomas who affirms that all of this history of love is enclosed in the Mass, because the eucharistic liturgy *"contains the whole mystery of our salvation"* (St. Thomas III, q 83, a 40).

The Mass is the memorial of what Jesus did when he came to look for us in order to save us. He *"gave"* himself for our sins: he sacrificed himself, died and is risen. The Mass revives this reality, which encompasses the entire meaning to our lives and which must become its focal point.

GOD GATHERS HIS PEOPLE

Maikona is a locality of the diocese of Marsabit in the middle of the desert: stretches of sand and vulcanic rock. Actually, Maikona is a well, which attracts a great number of nomads. Lines of camels line up daily towards the water, awaiting their turn with discipline.

In 1965, the bishop, far-sighted, opened up a missionary center right next to the well. Why right next to the well, if Maikona was not even a permanent village? The fact is that the camels are watered every two weeks. The missionary would meet the shepherds, who would arrive with their camels, every two weeks. The same people every two weeks; different people every day from the whole vast area. The missionary was able to cure them, instruct them and teach them the Gospel.

It can now be said that all of the Gabbra know the history of salvation and even a beautiful Christian community has been constituted amongst them.

I recently paid a visit to Maikona on a weekend.

During the whole Saturday morning the Christians continued to arrive and to camp with their camels around the church. The tent city grew throughout the whole afternoon and the evening. Others arrived on Sunday morning. Then, the celebration of the Mass began: a very lively feast due to the intensity of the participation, with drums, dances, and typical processions of their culture. No hurry at all, and so much joyous faith!

After the Mass, silence once again invaded the place. The priest had presented some Christians to me: *"This one walked for six hours. This one for eight hours. And they never miss it"*.

I shaked those dried up hands with admiration and I seemed to understand what the Mass was all about.

I was living a lively image once again: from the dispersion to the *"gathered church"*. Just as John motivates Jesus' sacrifice, that *"He had to die, in order to gather God's scattered children in unity"* (John 11:51-52).

Nobody finds himself living on the earth by chance. Jeremiah (Cfr. Jeremiah 31:3) assures us that everybody has been loved from eternity. We still did not exist, and we were already loved! Isaiah assures us that everybody is even called by name and counts in the Creator's eyes (Cfr. Isaiah 43:4). We are the fruit of a history of love and no day should be obscured by depression or by a bad mood. These moods arrive only if this 'history', which is better called *'HISTORY OF SALVATION'*, is forgotten.

It is not however so evident that life is a vocation, that is that we are called by God's love to exist, to be redeemed, to belong no less than to the divine community. The experience of sin has dulled all of this reality. *"Reading life as a vocation"* is a slogan made up by Card. Martini and we have to place ourselves in this school.

We form ourselves patiently and we rebuild ourselves at Mass as God has always thought of us.

The Mass in fact is the celebration of the paschal mystery, where "dead and resurrected" with Jesus Christ we respond to our vocation. Where, that is, called by God, we are led back to Him from the dispersion.

The whole Eucharist proclaims it and fulfills it.

An element of the rite continually reminds us of it: the assembly. The gathering of believers around the altar has a much more wider meaning than the simple obedience of the Church's precept. In fact, where two or more are gathered Jesus and therefore the Church is there (cfr. Matthew 18:20). The assembly, even if it is made up of a limited number of faithful – at least two! – represents the whole Church (Cfr. Sacrosanctum Concilium 2;7;26) and even all of humanity. A truly significant representation!

When we gather for Mass, we must become aware with joyous faith of what the assembly expresses. It declares ours and all of humanity's intimate vocation. Why do we gather? Not due to a recall of habit, of observance required of us or of the bell which has rung out... We are here because we have heard the call and we have understood human history as the history of salvation.

We are here because Jesus, right now, is gathering the dispersed children of God in unity. We do not remain in our rooms and in our homes: we come out!

Individualism and egoism are expressions of sin and are the characteristic of the old man, who still has to be redeemed. The assembly gives witness instead to human sociality, communion, unity: the Church.

Looking at people gathered together for the Mass is already contemplating the new humanity, no longer in competition, divided or even fighting amongst each other. The Jewish people in Egypt was enslaved, dispersed, deprived of its human and spiritual dignity; after having crossed the waters of the Red Sea it understood that it was an authentic people with its own laws, structures and freedom, but above all a people called to enjoy the *"new and eternal Covenant"* offered by God.

The Mass turns us into a 'body'. We are called to be the *"Body of Christ"*.

RUN AND CLARIFY THE WORLD

The oral tradition of the Borana, a nomadic tribe of Marsabit, could be entitled *"In the beginning was the Book"*. The ethnological sciences would find it very interesting and a study of extraordinary curiosity would result from it. The Boranas hand it down amongst themselves jealously, especially with the initiation of the youth. They do not say anything to strangers unless they are considered members of the tribe in some way. Maybe I deserved some regard, because an elderly friend of mine spoke to me about it many times.

In the beginning humanity belonged to a sole tribe, centered upon the progenitor Borée (who would correspond to Adam). The richness of this time and the reason for such a unity was due to the Book, which the first human group possessed. The word Book has an emblematic meaning and says much more than a simple reading object, given that nobody had ever learnt to read and to write. The Book was like a divine presence and made everything go well. But a mishap took place one day, when the cattle devoured the Book. For a people of shepherds this is very eloquent: the cattle, very rare in the desert, are considered as a great source of riches, almost as something sacred. From this event they dated all of the tragedies on the face of the earth. The greatest was the break-up of humanity, which disintegrated and then divided itself into innumerable tribes, with incommunicability due to the different languages and totally different interests. Borée remained with a handful of faithful followers, the Borana shepherds to be precise, but they too impoverished and self-centred. Wellbeing, the fertility of the land and the fertility of the animals were put at stake. There were terrible aberrations, so much so that even worshippers of Satan, tribes that practice sacrifices to evil spirits could be counted. The Ayana, for example, who even lived in the desert.

Fortunately there is a promise, handed down from time immemorial: a salvation will arrive and the Book will above all return. This is asserted by the Borana prophets, who read these things in the blood and in the intestines of the cattle, during periodic sacrifices.

The Book is the beginning is humanity's hope and around it humanity will find unity, peace and progress again.

They spread the news that the Father, having come from afar, was in possession of the Book and this created an extraordinary atmosphere of interest and of acceptance. Not that it was easy to assimilate the message of 'this' Book or that it was painless to move onto Christ's discipleship from atavistic customs, which contained positive and negative values. But the Book's fame fascinated everybody and the number of the first catechumens was very vast.

I saw Jesus' and even my mission being carried out: *"The Spirit of the Lord is upon me: he has sent me to proclaim the Good News"* (Luke 4:18). And later on, the Pope's words did a lot of good to me: *"Life is suspended between two heights: the Word and the Eucharist. The Word of God is the point of departure, a Word which calls, which invites, which personally questions, as had happened to the Apostles. When a person is reached by the Word, obedience, that is the listening which changes life, is born. At the culmination of this praying experience is the Eucharist, the other height indissolubly tied to the Word in so far as a place in which the Word makes itself flesh and blood"* (Orientale Lumen 10).

The Eucharist would have been too mysterious for quite some time (the catechumenate was foreseen for a period of at least four years); but the Word comes first. Truly: *"In the beginning was He who is the Word"* (John 1:1.14.18).

Recently, during a preaching, I met Matilde, a grandmother, all faith and wisdom. She had a worry, however: her little granddaughter, very lively and well prepared, notwithstanding her eight years of age, she still cannot receive the eucharistic communion. Matilde believes so much in the power of the Eucharist, that she finds it to be terrible that in that diocese children are admitted to Communion only during the last year of elementary school. But she has now discovered the Word and the Lectio Divina. She was radiant when she came to talk to me: *"The Church admits to having always venerated the Word as the Body of Christ, never ceasing to nourish itself at the only table of the Word and of the eucharistic Body* (Cfr. Dei Verbum 21). *My little granddaughter can't receive Communion; but she can receive the Word! The way must be quickly found for her to have it in an adequate way, at the appropriate age"*.

It is true, the Word comes first. In fact the Eucharist belongs to the so called 'mystagogy', that is to the baptized person's mature life. The Word is typical of the catechumen: it reaches him, it transforms him, it turns him into a believer and finally into a eucharistic Christian.

Even during the first centuries all of the disciples would gather together for the sanctification of the feast; but the catechumens would be dismissed after the liturgy of the Word. This was their nourishment: the other sacraments would await the day of baptism.

Gababo Guyò was a young Borana. Something of him will return in the following narratives. Right from the beginning the Spirit magnetized him and he would go around the incipient mission.

One day he stopped in front of me. He had a beautiful and honest smile. He asked me without beating around the bush to talk to him about this new religion which fascinated him a lot. Catechumenate still could not be talked of, because everything was just beginning; but we would chat and read some initial pages of the Book almost every evening. Then the first catechumenate was able to take off with a considerable group of friends. Then, a real daily lesson could be held and it always consisted in a page of the Old and then of the New Testament.

One day Gababo confided to me: *"The Book is very beautiful and everyday I await with joy for the moment of the meeting. I think to myself everyday:*

Today the father has read the most beautiful page of the Book. But you read an even more beautiful one the day after!".

The listening of the word generates the biblical mentality: to *"reason like God"* (Matthew 16:23).

Some time ago there was a liturgical aid, a monthly booklet which carried the daily readings of the eucharistic liturgy. It had as a title: *"At Mass"*. It even carried sober notes, well done. It wanted to be for everybody, to be kept at home!

I gave it as a gift to a six year old girl, Antonella. She hardly knew how to read, but she had the true spirit of the evangelical child. Every evening, after the news on television, she herself would go to turn the television off and would sweetly invite, with a certain pride, her parents and grandparents to listen. In front of them, she would proclaim, or at least syllabize, the Gospel of the day. She was very proud of her booklet. The effects were not long in verifying themselves: a lot of peace in the family, a growing faith, an availability to noteworthy physical trials supported with strength and dignity!

The Word sets off and brings about mission. It has to 'run and clarify' the world.

"When this word is preached, by means of the preacher's voice, it gives his voice, which is perceived exter-

nally, the virtue of working internally, therefore the dead acquire life once again and are reborn in the joy of the sons of Abraham.

This word is therefore alive in the Father's heart, alive on the preacher's mouth, alive in the heart of whoever believes and whoever loves. And exactly because this word is so alive, there's no doubt that it is even efficacious" (Balduin of Canterbury).

The Word carries out its work as if travelling along a route, from heaven to us. In the ancient community of Alexandria of Egypt, Clement and Origin called it *"Lectio Divina"*: they above all lived it out with the faithful, who then knew a time of fervent liveliness and of readiness for martyrdom. Around 1,150 A.D., Guigo the Carthusian described the way of the Lectio Divina in the five stages *(Lectio, Meditatio, Oratio, Contemplatio, Communicatio),* which after the Second Vatican Council are once again becoming the prescribed path for the personal and collective evangelization of the men called to become sons of God.

The Word is not only to be proclaimed in the eucharistic liturgy: it is the life of everyone who listens to it.

Matthew asked me an embarrasing question one day, while he was playing with his three other little brothers. I was talking to his parents, who probably had made it a matter of our conversation. And he, interrupting the game, asked me: *"But what is the Lectio Divina?"*.

What could I say to a 9 year old child, all intent on noisy and lively games? I got around to babbling: *"Lectio Divina is this: you listen to one of Jesus' words and you become that word"*. Matthew ran away to play; but something was working in his little mind, because every now and then he would run to ask me: *"Give me an example"*. And the example became a game in turn. From time to time I would tell him: *"God tells you: I love you* (Cfr. Isaiah 43:4), *and you are sure of it for the rest of your life". God tells you: Do not fear* (Cfr. Isaiah 43:1.5) *and you never ever fear"*. This worried him and he wanted to assure himself if it even went for the night. *"Jesus tells you: Blessed are the pure in heart"* (Cfr. Matthew 5:8). *"Jesus tells you: Blessed are those who aren't violent"* (Cfr. Matthew 5:5). This worried him once again because after a while he came to tell me: *"But I don't have all that much patience!"*. I took the cue in order to subsequently explain to him: *"But this is precisely the Lectio Divina: Jesus does not only order you from afar to be patient; but he gives it to you as a gift. The word comes to live in you"*. He liked this. When we said goodbye to each other, he assured me: *"If Jesus has given me patience, from now on I will no longer treat my little brother with roughness, I will no longer bang the doors, I will no longer answer back to my mother when she asks me to help her around the home".*

The same thing happened to Mary. *"She said: Your word be done in me"* (Luke 1:38). And the Word went to live in her!

If only we were to take the proclamation of the Word like this at Mass!

THE MASS TRANSFORMS
THE WORLD

Venceslaa is now an elderly missionary sister in Colombia. I knew her since when she was a young nun and directed some works of a big community. It was back then that she taught me a beautiful thing about the Mass.

I would observe her with admiration: she had a lot of things to do, but she would move around the whole day with a splendid smile and a fine availability. Things did not always went well; in fact, a very sad episode, fortunately known only to a few, took place in the community. She was aware of it, and yet she continued to smile and to serve as if nothing had happened. I wanted to talk to her about it: *"How do you always manage to keep yourself serene, even during difficult moments?"*. She answered me: *"It's the Mass, father!"*.

And she told me:

"When I was twelve years old a retreat was held in the parish. The preacher talked about the Mass. He

explained the rite of the drops of water in the chalice at the offertory. The drops of water are so insignificant that they lose themselves in the wine.

We can say that they become wine. When the priest offers the chalice he doesn't mention them anymore: 'Blessed are you, Lord, for this wine'. Now, the evangelist John makes it understood that the wine recalls the divine nature and the water human nature. In John's footsteps the Fathers of the Church have followed this symbolism: the wine recalls the Eternal Word, the water the humanity assumed; the wine the Redeemer, the water redeemed humanity; the wine Jesus the head, the water men who are members of his body; the wine Jesus, the water the assembly and each one of the participants.

This doctrine dazzled me. From that day onwards I was no longer able to miss one Mass. I lived three kilometers away from the church, in the countryside. The road wasn't paved and at times it could be muddy. The celebration would take place at sunrise, so that farmers and workers could participate in it before going to work. But every morning, in the dark, on my bicycle, I had to go there: I was too interested in being one of the little drops of water. It would happen that at times I would be distracted before or after, but never during that moment. And all of this sustained me. The joys and difficulties don't belong to me and are taken by Jesus".

It isn't a children's story. The Council of Trent itself (Session XXI, chap. 7) sees the water in the wine just like the Fathers of the Church have seen it and talks of sinful humanity's renewal which becomes holy.

Of course, at times, the priest's gestures which accompany that ceremony can pass by unobserved, overlapped as they often are to other movements, done quickly and maybe hidden to the eyes of the faithful by candlesticks and by flowers. For me it had been at length like this. The efficacy of the liturgy even depends on knowledge and on participation. *"In the liturgy, the signs speak"*. The merit of the Second Vatican Council had even been that of indicating the Mass to us as the *"summit and the source of all Christian life"* (*Sacrosanctum Concilium* 10; *Lumen Gentium* 11; *Apostolicam Actuositatem* 9; *Christus Dominus* 30; *Presbyterorum Ordinis* 5; 6; 14).

The way of personal and ecclesial renewal is the eucharist. The whole Mass affirms it and carries it out: it expresses it adequately and it marvelously puts it into effect (Cfr. *Lumen Gentium* 11).

What happens with the water in the wine is the consequence of the sacrifice which makes us the body of Christ according to the new and eternal covenant. The transformation touches its height in the communion.

Humanity is a creature. It's a small reality, but in the mystery of the divine participation it becomes infinitely big! It is in God's style *"the disproportion between the very humble means which he uses and the great things which he does"* (Tertullian).

All of us experience inside a yearning need to change and to become better. At birth, gracious and cuddled children, we are called by the word of God *"children of anger"* (Ephesians 2:3) and *"old man"* (Colossians 3:9; Ephesians 4:22). We cannot really save ourselves on our own. What is more, every day all of us would like to unload the heavy burden of miseries and of mistakes off us. Renew oneself, change and grow are inner laws of life. By ourselves we wouldn't really know how to move ourselves.

But we have the Mass!

There is no space for renunciations or discouragement: all that has to be done is to assume the humility of the insignificant drops of water and believe that the *"children of anger"* in Jesus the Son become children of God, and that *"the old man"* in Jesus the New Man becomes a new man.

The Church has really found the way of renewal and of transformation!

ONE ONLY BODY

Menennio Agrippa, in order to try to halt the crumbling of Roman society, narrated the famous *"apologue"* to the plebes. Even if this took place many years before Christ, the words of the noble patrician however remain current.

The apologue sounds like this: the members of the human body; tired of continuously working for the functioning of one sole organism, rebelled. Every member said: *"I am no longer going to be the servant of others"*. And so the hand refused to take food to the mouth, the mouth stopped chewing, the stomach stopped digesting. However, they had to capitulate very soon and recognize that they were each made for each other. And they once again decided to collaborate.

St. Paul returned to this image and he edited it in the Word of God. Not only once but with constant references:

✶ Romans 12:5: *"Just like in one only body we have many members, the same with us; being many, we are one body in Christ"*.

✶ 1 Corinthians 12:12.27: *"All of the members, though being many, are one only body, as it is with Christ. ... You together are Christ's body"*.

✶ Ephesians 4:4: *"One only body, one only spirit, just as there is only one hope to which you have been called, that of your vocation"*.

✶ Acts 9 (Cfr. Galatians 1:12 and Acts 8:3) tell of an episode of Paul's life. While he was going to Damascus, equipped with a letter that authorized him to arrest Christians, falling on the ground, he felt himself asked: *"Why are you persecuting me?"*. And who was introduced him questioning himself: *"I am that Jesus whom you're persecuting"*. But Paul only persecuted Christian men and women. The passage was logical: Jesus and that people identified themselves in only one *"Body"*.

It had been Jesus who had given a definitive revelation of it. We have to speak of revelation because it cannot be either intuitable, or even less, realizable by human means. We, by ourselves, are rather capable of individualism and of division. We can, at the most, arrive at partial gestures of service and of friendship; but unity is fulfilled by Jesus: he came and died in order to *"gather the dispersed*

41

sons of God in unity" (John 11:52). Therefore it is an already fulfilled fact.

In order to make the concept of unity understandable to the disciples, Jesus has recourse to a rural image: *"I am the vine, you are the branches"* (John 15:5). It is not thinkable that a branch can live cut off from the vine and from solidarity with the other branches.

He had expressed it in many other ways. The most solemn is in prayer addressed to the Father, with whom unity is perfect and unique: *"Father, that they may be one like us"* (John 17:11.21.23).

In its incarnation the eternal Word had 'married' humanity: *"With the omnipotent having taken a weak woman as a bride and the Most High one of a lower condition, He turned her into a queen from a slave ... The bridegroom therefore is united with the Father ... Like the head and the body form only one man, so the Son of the Virgin and his elected members constitute only one man, the only Son of man. According to Scripture, the total and integral Christ is both head and body"* (Isaac of the Star).

The Eucharist reassumes in itself this revelation which Jesus pronounces on the bread: *"This is my body"*. He has fulfilled perfect unity between himself and us: we, significant in the bread, which was in the ears of wheat, swaying on the hills, reaped, harvested, threshed, then in the grains, milled,

42

becoming wheat, pervaded by yeast, baked in the oven!

The bread, which represents us, becomes strongly symbolic and embraces all of our reality:

* *It is a fragrant bread* – the pleasant odour, the taste, the beauty represent all of the positive aspects of our existence. We have so many joys, successes, values which can very well find themselves in the bread's fragrance.

* *It is a baked bread* – In order to become bread, the grains have suffered, they have been crushed at the mill, they have been kneaded and introduced into the oven. They have paid the price. Therefore all of human life tastes suffering. All of our sufferings find a confirmation in the bread.

* *It is a bread that has been worked* – Our lives are above all toil, just like the bread is a symbol of work. One toils 'in order to earn his own bread'. Every success in the material, intellectual and spiritual field requires commitment and dedication.

* *It is a gathered bread* – The table is really the symbol of the family and of friendship. The bread is really born of the gathering and of the fusion of the grains.

Many have collaborated in its production: there are those who have selected the seeds, those who have thrown them into the furrows, those who have cultivated the plant, those who have caressed and gathered the ears, those who have threshed, those who have milled, kneaded, baked, distributed... Just like the bread signifies unity, so we, the grains, live together in unity.

And upon this significant bread Jesus carries out his transforming work: *"This is my body"*. Heaven and earth become only one body. And for this reason we're in the world!

In the encyclical *"Mystical Body"* of Pius XII (Mystici Corporis 60-64) a surprising affirmation is contained: the unity amongst the members of Christ's body is infinitely superior to that of the members of the human body. These last ones are connected by four ties: skeleton, muscles, nerves and circulatory system. The tie between two baptized people is the Trinity itself! We have God in common. It is surprising, but even perfectly obvious.

It is a reality worked by God: to us the task of discovering it and living it out.

We are therefore *"one"*. We are the body of Christ.

CONSANGUINITY

Today there is AIDS. Blood can no longer be fooled around with. A secret association in China, described as a kind of mafia sect, recently modified the oath of affiliation which was sealed with blood. The members would mix some drops of the initiate's blood into a chalice and they would pass it around from mouth to mouth. AIDS dissuaded them from practicing this insidious rite and now each one lightly wounds his own body and assumes his own blood.

When Kenya underwent the guerilla war of the Mau-Mau, who were fighting for the independence of the country from British colonialism, in the 1950's and 1960's, the blood oath was adopted. The revolutionaries committed themselves with it and invited the people to adhere to it by doing the same. Christians held this oath as illicit and even an apostasy, because the revolution contained violence and hate and even proposed the return to paganism. As if getting freedom back comprised of a return to the original culture. An incompatible oath with baptism, therefore. Christians were often physically forced to drink the blood of the oath and there was a significant number of martyrs who resisted at the cost of their lives. Many however believed in the force of the oath imposed: the force of the blood was such that it seemed to conquer the free choice of baptism. After the attainment of independence, it was a truly missionary enterprise to put order back even into ideas.

The oath of blood, therefore, is even found again in present history and it isn't a prerogative of the oriental peoples of antiquity.

When God spoke to humanity, he chose Abraham and his culture as interlocutors. Through Abraham, he announced his plan of salvation and offered to the Jewish people his covenant. On that occasion, God adopted the oath of blood, which was then a solemn and widespread practice. Lips were moistened with the blood of animal and, at times, human victims. Sometimes the contracting parties would wound their forearms and would draw the wounds together, almost giving their blood reciprocally from vein to vein.

Genesis talks about it. Chapter 15 states that *"The Lord made this covenant with Abraham"*, asking him to quarter a certain number of animals, in the midst of which *"a fuming oven and a burning flame passed"*.

Chapters 19 and 24 of Exodus refer to how God sealed the covenant with Moses: *"Moses built an altar with twelve stones for the twelve tribes of Israel. He entrusted some youths with the task of slaughtering steers as a sacrifice of communion with the Lord. Moses took the book of the covenant and he read it in the presence of the people. They said: We will do and we'll carry out what the Lord has ordered us! Moses took the blood and sprinkled the people, saying: Here is the blood of the covenant that the Lord has concluded with us"*.

It was a covenant between God and humanity. It was renewed many times over. Abraham and Moses erected altars in perennial memory.

Eucharistic prayer IV notes that God *"offered his covenant to men many times"*.

Jeremiah addresses his glance to all of these opportunities, which generally have failed due to human blindness, and foresees a new era: *"I will form a new covenant. Deep within them I will put my law, I will write it upon their hearts. I will be their God and they will be my people!"* (Jeremiah 31:33).

The *"new and eternal"* covenant will come about in Jesus. *"The mystery is Christ in you"* (Colossians 1:27). No longer victims and blood of creatures: the efficacious victim is the eternal incarnate Word. It's the 'divine' victim and, at the same time, the priest.

Chapters 7-10 of the Letter to the Hebrews describe him like this: *"Jesus became the guarantor of a better covenant. He entered once and for all into the sanctuary, not with the blood of goats and of calves, but with his own blood, after having obtained an eternal redemption for us. He has now appeared in order to annul sin by means of the sacrifice of himself. With a sole oblation he has made those who are sanctified perfect forever. Thus having full trust to enter into the sanctuary by means of Jesus' blood, by this new and living way let us approach God with a sincere heart in the fullness of faith"*.

Jesus, perfect God and perfect man, carries out in himself God's encounter with humanity. In Him, the Trinity. In Him, humanity. In Him, therefore, the covenant.

The Gospel reports his words: "I ardently desired to eat this passover with you". And taking a chalice, gave thanks and said: *"Take it and distribute it amongst yourselves. This chalice is the new covenant in my blood, which is poured out for you"* (Luke 22:15-20).

St. Paul resumes: *"Is not the chalice of blessing which we bless a communion with Christ's blood?"* (1 Corinthians 10:16).

In the Mass, the formula of the consecration affirms: *"Blood of the new and eternal covenant"*.

According to the oriental, ancient and modern mentality, blood is the source of life and it signifies life. For the Orientals, therefore, exchanging blood in the oath is equal to exchanging life. As if they were saying: *"Your blood has come to flow in my veins and mine in yours. As a result, your life has passed to me, mine to you"*. It is unthinkable to break an oath: it would equal betraying oneself, more than the other person.

Analogously, Jesus defined communion: *"Whoever eats my flesh and drinks my blood lives in me and I live in him"* (John 6:56).

St. Cyprian, admired, would look at the faithful leaving the eucharistic assembly: *"I see your lips drenched by the blood of Christ!"*. He would see the creatures inhabited by the Creator.

GOD AND MAN ALLIED

As a missionary in the desert of Marsabit, I even learned to pray from pagans.

Gababo Guyò had been the first person to ask to become a Christian. Right from the first steps he remained absorbed by the Spirit.

Having finished work in the late afternoon we would sit on the sand and read some passages from the first pages of the Bible. Then I would retire to the temporary hut which we dared call church and my friends would return to their homes.

Gababo loved to pause even himself in prayer, nestling himself close to the entrance.

One evening he yelled behind me: *"Father, teach me how to pray"*. I objected because I saw him in church everyday, but he explained to me: *"I do not know how to pray anymore. When I begin, I have so many things to ask for: the earth is burned by the drought, the camels often contract illnesses, the tribes are continuously fighting amongst themselves, my mother has become old and is having a hard time gathering wood for the fire… But now I no longer want to make requests to the Lord and for this reason I'm asking you to teach me how to pray".* I insisted: *"But in the meantime you continue to spend a lot of time in church. What are you doing?".* He answered me: *"Some days ago you read in the Book the story of Abraham who met the Lord and about their covenant. Abraham was so happy about it that he erected a stone altar. But even you have built a stone altar and, when you're in front of it, I think: God and the father meet: God is here and sees our needs without us having to communicate them to him. So I stay there, happy that God seals a covenant with you and even with me. It seems very beautiful to me, but I don't know how to say anything to him. In those moments time flies away very fast. The fatigue of a day of work vanishes. I don't even feel malaria any longer".* Gababo had his eyes full of light.

I told him: *"Continue to do this. This is true prayer. I too want to pray like you!".*

Gababo – still a pagan, we can say – taught his missionary how the covenant is lived out. There are no adequate words to express what God offers to his little ones. We're overwhelmed, transformed and happy. And there's God who floods human history.

The words which we listen to at Mass, at the moment of the consecration of the chalice: *"... New and eternal covenant"* explain human history, unveil the meaning of life and describe the gift which we have received. They are synonyms of the three aspects *"Mystery-Communion-Mission"*, used in the exhortation *'PASTORES DABO VOBIS'* in order to signify the journey and the content of the faith.

In politics allies work together and share (or should share!) prosperity and dangers. God's allies are called to live the earthly adventure in divine peace and in the understanding of participating in the Trinity's life.

Mass, communion and the continuous eucharistic presence are the cornerstones of our faith! The word *"covenant"* expresses all of the history of salvation: the mercy of God needs to be contemplated in it. The New Testament affirms with solemnity that *"God is love"* (1 John 4:16). We will understand it better in paradise. Down here we only have pale images of God's love for us.

Above all, the Lord assures us of the covenant and He offers it: *"Here, I establish a covenant: in the presence of all the people I will work wonders, which were never worked in any other country and in any other nation"* (Exodus 34:10).

The covenant is similar to a dialogue: *"The Lord spoke with Moses face to face, like a man speaks to another man".*

Even more, it's like a wedding: *"Like a young man who marries a bride, so your Creator will marry you; as the groom rejoices over the bride, so your God will rejoice over you"* (Isaiah 62:5; cfr. Isaiah 54:5).

Let us now analyze God's paternity. Jesus says: *"Your Father who is in heaven"* (Matthew 6:26). We read also: *"My father and my mother have abandoned me, but the Lord has welcomed me"* (Psalm 26:6). *"Does a woman ever forget her child, so as to not concern herself for the child of her womb? Even if there were a woman who were to forget, I instead will never forget you"* (Isaiah 49:14; cfr. Isaiah 66:13). *"Is not Ephraim a dear son to me, a chosen child of mine?"* (Jeremiah 31:20).

Love, *"which has not allowed God to remain alone"* (St. Thomas) and led him into creating the universe and made him a redeemer: *"Rejoice, Israel: the Lord your God in your midst is a powerful saviour"* (Zephaniah 3:15). His heart is *"rich in mercy"* towards sinful man. *"Even if the mountains were to move themselves and the hills to waver, my affection wouldn't distance itself from you, nor would my covenant of peace waver – says the Lord who shows mercy to you"*

(Isaiah 54:10). And Zephaniah goes as far as to affirm: *"He will rejoice with you with cries of joy, like on feast days"* (3:18).

The New Testament expresses the covenant by means of many other words. Especially by means of *"unity"* and *"communion"*. It, moreover, uses a splendid synthesis: *"I am in the Father, you in Me and I in you"* (John 14:20).

WE BECOME WHAT WE RECEIVE

Heresy has always knocked on the door of Christian life, right from apostolic times. But for about a thousand years nobody dared formulate any doubt, given that revelation's words are so clear (Cfr. Luke 22:14-23; Matthew 26:26-30; Mark 14:22-26; 1 Corinthians 11:23-25). After 1000, a certain Berengarius of Tours began to ask himself how Jesus' affirmations on his presence as eucharistic bread had to be interpreted. Is it a question of a *"real"* or *"symbolic"* presence? Defenders of the faith arose from everywhere and many works were written in defense of tradition. A booklet was written by a holy abbot, Guitmond of Aversa, in 1073, with the title: *"De corporis et sanguinis Christi libri tres (The three books about the Body and Blood of Christ)"*.

A pleasant and lively page is drawn from it.

In the Middle Ages academic questions were in style, and curious facts would not infrequently happen. Let us imagine a very modest church, lost in the fields, and a really poor tabernacle, made up of four little planks of wood and inside of it, upon a plate, the consecrated bread. A mouse, climbing up onto the tabernacle, could easily chew away at the wood and ... even at the consecrated bread. On the sacred doctors' agenda, even this question appeared amongst the various others: *"Did the mouse have communion?"*.

One can laugh about it. But what should be said about all of those communions which we receive without them provoking any change in faith, in brotherly love, in the observance of the word of God?

A mouse does not establish any relationship of love. The mouse's communion is too common, too easy! Just as common and easy can be the sign of the cross, genuflection and the recitation of prayers if they are carried out without due emotional participation.

One could comment: *"What a shame! Nothing happened"*. But St. Paul doesn't think about it this way, when he examines believers' condition of mediocrity and spiritual death and refers its cause to not *"discerning the Body of Christ"*. For St. Paul, a communion that does not discern the Body of Christ is very negative: *"They eat their own condemnation"* (1 Corinthians 11:29).

The 'mouse's communion' must constitute an admonition not to allow Christian life to get itself lost in indifference and in habit. The stake at play is really very high.

However, what can fascinate us and magnetize all of our need to live in a Christian way is the eucharistic event in its positive meaning. A central event in history which gives a meaning to life.

Salvation history flows into man's deification: we are creatures called to share in God's life. This gift is already granted to us even on earth through the Eucharist.

Pope St. Leo I already taught it, in the fifth century, by writing: *"When we go to communion, we become what we receive"*. The Second Vatican Council has appreciated these meaningful words and has incorporated them into its documents for the catechesis of modern times (Cfr. Lumen Gentium 26).

St. Leo echoes St. Augustine who attributes very similar words to Jesus: *"You will not change me in you, but I will change you in me"*.

The man of the mythical Prometheus tried in a sacrilegious way to climb to heaven. This expresses man's most deepest expectation; but it cannot be an enterprise of ours, because only God can transform us. And He transforms us in communion!

Jesus himself described the event like this: *"Whoever eats my flesh and drinks my blood lives in me and I live in him"* (John 6:56). They are words that ought to be pondered at length. No intelligence whatsoever can understand this affirmation. Intelligence can only admit that nothing any higher can be said on earth: God in man!

Card. Ratzinger comments: *"'Communion' means that the apparently impassable barrier of my I is shattered. It is shattered because Jesus first of all wanted to open up all of himself, he has welcomed all of us inside of himself and has given himself totally to us. 'Communion' therefore means the fusion of existences..."* (The Church, p. 25).

The history of salvation calls itself communion and deifies baptized man both from his existence on earth to his everlasting life.

The Second Vatican Council has therefore rightly defined Eucharist as the "peak and source" of all life, placed at the center of existence as the content of Christian formation and strategy of the tension towards holiness.

WE ARE THE BODY OF CHRIST

"You hide yourself from the wise and you reveal your-self to the little ones" (Luke 10:21). Jesus said it familiarly to the Father, upsetting our human way of talking. An exceptional lesson.

I noticed it, at my own expenses, when John came to me with a letter in his hand: *"It's my mother's birthday: would you like to sign?"*. I willingly added my best wishes and gave the letter back; but John would not move: *"Aren't you going to read?"*. He had written: *"Mum, your birthday falls on such and such a day, but we are so far away... You, however, go to communion on that day and receive Jesus and me; I'll go to communion and I'll receive Jesus and you. Isn't this how we celebrate your birthday together?"*. It seemed too high a concept for me and I babbled: *"How do you dare write these things to your mother?"*. With a familiar attitude, John gave me a nudge: *"Didn't we meditate them together last week, reading St. Augustine and St. Leo the Great?"*.

59

It was true. He, with a child's pure spirit, had welcomed them and had lived them out, while I, in my intellectualism, had deeply tasted them, but had stored them in my knowledge. I then noticed myself reacting like this in front of theological affirmations. John is in the right and he testifies how communion is lived out.

St. Paul had affirmed it: *"Given that there is only one bread, we, though being many, are one only body: we all in fact participate of the one bread"* (1 Corinthians 10:17). St. Leo the Great had echoed him, quoted by the Second Vatican Council (Lumen Gentium 26): *"The participation in the body and blood of Christ does not do anything else but change us into what we receive"*. St. Augustine interrogated his faithful one day: *"What do you see on the altar?"*. *"The sacrament"*. *"The sacrament (= sign) of who? Of Christ or of us?"*. *"Of us"*. The faithful of Hipponia re-echoed the prayer of the Didaké: *"Lord, this bread was first wheat in the wavering ears of wheat on the hills. It has been gathered, milled and baked into the one bread. Gather us in the same way"*.

When we say *"Amen"* to the Body of Christ which the priest presents to us at communion, we even have to recognize the human community. It is all there, gathered in unity by Jesus. Not even one person can be left out, not even an 'enemy', because the Body of Christ is so unitary that by renouncing even one member can make us run the risk of rejecting the whole body. That holy bread is really a sign of the presence of all of humanity. The family, the community, all of society are signified in it. Communion is the strong moment of fraternal love. We welcome each other 'inside'. Just as Jesus affirmed: *"Whoever eats... lives in me and I in him"*.

At the moment of communion, parents, brothers, children live their familiar intimacy in the greatest tenderness possible. The same thing happens for every community and for the whole Church. Even at a distance, because mystical unity knows no distance, a purely physical concept.

In the Body of Christ there is more than meeting; there is fusion.

There exists no prayer that gets me into God and distances myself from others, or which even neglects others. As St. Dorothy of Gaza efficaciously writes: *"Imagine that the earth is a circle... Imagine that this circle is the world and that the center of the circle is God. If men move from the circle towards the center wishing to get close to God, as they proceed they get close to God and they get close to each other. And the more they get close to each other, the more they get close to God"*.

MASS BECOMES MISSION

A scholarship for the university of Rome was offered to a young Indian doctor, a Hindu and deeply religious: he would have been able to specialize himself in surgery. There was no surgeon in his city. He was very happy about it, evidently for the specialization, but even for a religious reason: he would have met people of other religions and he would have been able to pray with them. It is a cultural and eclectic note common to the Hindus. For them all religions are equally valid and all of them, in different ways, lead to the same goal. No religion can pretend to be the only true one and as a result there is no reason in converting oneself from one to another. Even Gandhi, who admired Christ and made the discourse of the mountain his own, saw it this way but he never thought about becoming a Christian and condemned the work of Catholic missionaries. It is read in a Hindu book: *"The Chri-*

stian must not become a Hindu, nor a Buddhist. A Hindu, or a Buddhist, must not become a Christian. Each one has to assimilate each other's spirit and maintain at the same time one's own individuality" (Vivekananda).

During the trip, our doctor entered into the mosques and prayed with the Muslims. He met Jews and wanted to pray with them in the synagogues. In Rome, he promised himself once again to pray even with Christians. He did not know anything about Christianity. He only realized that Christians at times gathered themselves in particularly beautiful buildings, in order to pray together.

It was like this that on a Sunday he united himself to the crowd that entered into St. Andrew of the Valley. It was for Mass, but he didn't know anything about it. He was solely animated by a great attention of being able to pray with Christians. At a certain moment he saw everybody rummaging their pockets and offering money, while a procession moved itself from the back of the church: some bread and some vases were being brought, which the priest accepted and raised on the altar with great dignity. He thought: *"It seems that Christians, when they pray, give something"*.

He had not brought anything with him. He felt induced to make up for it with a prayer: *"Lord, I will work for the poor"*.

Now, having become a surgeon, he is in his native city, Madras, and he is the head of the hospital. He is famous for this: he does not give himself free time, and after his normal daily turn he still lags behind in his office in order to receive the poor, and he receives them free of charge!

The Holy Spirit had found the open way in order to communicate himself to him and in order to inspire him to offer the gift of himself.

This doctor teaches about participation: we do not go to Mass *"as foreigners or mute spectators"* (Sacrosanctum Concilium 47). But he above all teaches that the Mass projects itself upon our lives. The Hindu doctor was no longer as he was before: that Mass turned him into a missionary of love.

The Mass makes us *"an acceptable sacrifice to God"*, that is new people, touched by Him. The Mass has called us, it has transformed us and sends us. Mass and life; Mass and mission, therefore!

The experience of the Eucharist does not finish at one's exit through the door of Church after the celebration, but it 'goes' throughout the whole world. It has been said to us: *"The Mass is ended"*. Its genuine meaning is: *"The Mass is not over"*. *'Principles and Norms'* of the missal adverts: *"The assembly is dismissed so that each person returns to his occupations praising and blessing God"* (57). The eucharistic charge is such that it rediscovers its real name: mission.

It is the mission of peace, as the liturgical greeting suggests: *"Go in peace!"*.

The Word had announced: *"God has reconciled us with himself by means of Christ. He has reconciled the world to himself like this. Let yourselves be reconciled"* (2 Corinthians 5:18ff.). And the reconciliation has been abundantly bestowed upon us. A profound conversion has come about and a perfect communion with heaven and earth has been given to us.

The assembly has meant the joyous pacification of gathered humanity. The symbolism of the bread and of the wine – grains and grapes fused into unity – has spoken with the force of peace. Communion is even synonymous with peace: one becomes what he receives. Now: *"Christ is our peace!"*. Mass carries out Jesus' prayer: *"Father, that all may be one, just as you and I are one"* (John 17:21).

All of this is not carried out in a circumscribed time, while we're there, around the altar, but accompanies all of life. How would it be possible to define this action which is eternal and represents the foundation of all existence as 'over'?

Mission starts from there, just as Jesus said addressing himself to the Father: *"Just as you have sent me into the world, I too have sent them into the world"* (John 17:18).

The prayer after the Our Father seems to exactly describe this missionary eucharistic life:

✷ Free us, oh Lord from all evil,
✷ grant peace to our days
✷ and with the help of your mercy, we will always live free from sin and secure from all anxiety,
✷ as we wait that the blessed hope will be fulfilled and that our saviour Jesus Christ will come.

They are the most beautiful chapters of existence and, lived out in the family of God, they are at the same time a gift and a commitment of each person and a gift and a sharing of the community.

Whoever has lived out the Mass, still lives it out after the celebration. He is a carrier of peace: his words, his behaviour, his style of life continue to communicate peace. The 'missionary going' and the 'awaiting of the blessed hope' focus upon the destination: the going will not rest until the hope is carried out fully.

History is made up of those fascinating chapters and one of its names is mission. The Mass is a guarantee and a furnace of history and of mission.

Mass then is a missionary meeting, a departure strip, so that from day to day, by means of Christ, the mediator, we be fashioned into unity with God and amongst ourselves, so that God may finally be all in all (Cfr. *Sacrosanctum Concilium* 48).

RADIANT WITH THE TRINITY

My native town is crouched at the feet of the maritime Alps and for a brief period it had prospects of economic prosperity. The Montecatini factory had identified the presence of uranium in the rocks of the area and a work site arose. The revenue wasn't able to absorb the costs of the installations and everything ended within a few years. In the meantime many poor people had found work and bread.

Those mountaineers were not able to believe their own eyes: those rocks, which their flocks had always trampled, contained energy and wealth! Many took one of those rocks home with them in order to keep them as ornaments in their rooms. The fact was that there really was radioactivity and not few ended up in hospital with pulmonary problems. Just for a piece of rock!

I thought about these facts again, when reflecting upon the Eucharist in our lives, the approach became obvious. After Mass, even we are radioactive rocks.

God's presence on earth cannot be inert! He is always the same creator, redeemer, community in perennial and perfect mutual gift.

And now He's not immobilized by a metal or marble tabernacle. He said: *"Whoever eats... lives in me and I live in him"* (John 6:56). Mass has made of a sinner the heaven where God lives. Scripture never ceases repeating it: *"I no longer live; Christ lives in me"* (Galatians 2:20); *"You know that you are God's temple and that God's Spirit lives in you"* (1 Corinthians 3:16); *"God's Spirit lives in you"* (Romans 8:9;10;11). Exactly a fact and the realization of the most beautiful word: *"We will be our abode in him!"* (John 14:23).

A rock irradiating uranium. The rock remains that little heap of limestone which is trampled under one's feet, but nobody can stop the uranium: it irradiates!

Not even the Eucharist changes my appearance: it remains an insignificant reality. A little thing, Mary herself defined it as (cfr. Luke 1:48), a nothing, St. John of the Cross, and St. Augustine defined it as: a misery. A little creature. But at the same time I become God's house, which by moving allows only whoever lives in it to move.

If I dedicate myself to the apostolate, I am exactly like the ornament of the mountaineers of my town: above all, I am in front of my neighbour and I allow God to visit him. If I serve, whatever my service be, this is insignificant with regard to the irradiating power of He who lives and dwells in me. If I retire to the desert in order to love the whole mystical body at a time, it is always He who lives in me who irradiates himself upon the whole world.

I am impotent, and yet I'm mission itself. I do not count at all, and yet I am contagious and, through my nothingness, God communicates himself. I can be neglected by others, go by unobserved, be misunderstood and even maybe imprisoned, but nobody can stop the real life and real love.

And neither does the quality of my service count. Blessed Elizabeth of the Trinity, herself surprised, would say: *"There is no real difference between prayer and the laundry. There are no more unimportant things"!*

Mass leads us right here. We have been convoked, transformed and, now, sent. Mass is an hour of celebration and twenty-three of mission!

The Romans, an extremely democratic people, for everything that would regard civic life (= the re [thing] public) used to gather themselves in explicit buildings, called basilicas. They would propose, discuss, deliberate. An usher, at the end of the meeting, would announce the dissolving of the assembly: *"Ite, dimissio est"*. In the Latin declination, 'dimissio' became 'missio' and then 'missa'.

The church inferred from Roman antiquity both the architectural structure and the name of the people's place of encounter. It above all adopted the invitation to dissolve the assembly: it in fact wasn't any kind of dispersion, but a going to implement the decisions taken. The equivalence is precisely defined: the Romans would decide with regard to social life, from the cult to the market, to games, to public works... The consequent commitment regarded these sectors. Christians at Mass live out salvation history, 'they become what they receive', they found themselves in communion with the Trinity and with all of humanity. Their consequent commitment is mission!

Jesus pronounced the last word on the Mount of Olives, in the garden of the ascension: *"GO"*. The dissolving formula of the eucharistic assembly contains it.

We will really be irradiating rocks, then. Mass doesn't alienate us from the earth, but really does great things in us. In fact Eucharist means thanksgiving. We do not have sufficient words in order to give thanks for the divine presence, so 'different' from ours, and yet so much ours as to be able to communicate it to humanity. But the thanksgiving is in things: in the wonder and in the joy of living in God, right from our earthly days.

A RAISED SIGN AMONG
THE NATIONS
FOR THE SALVATION OF ALL

I had crossed the whole desert of Marsabit and I had reached a village on the border between Kenya and Ethiopia. A sympathetic shack of iron sheets was soon prepared and on the following day I wanted to go towards the village, in order to meet 'my people': it was for them that I had come!

They had told me that the majority of people were pagans and that there was a certain number of Muslims. A little white mosque soared amongst the poor huts. An Islamic feast occurred on that day and a certain number of young men were conducting a procession. They were coming towards me in order to then deviate towards some sacred place. They decisively walked, raising up a cloud of dust, and they sang with enthusiasm.

I was happy to meet them and I looked at them just like a shepherd looks over his flock. But they just passed by me, only intent upon their ceremony and their song. Nobody noticed me at all. And yet I was the first foreigner who came to establish himself amongst them: I certainly constituted a curiosity.

I had come to the desert animated by a sincere apostolic ardor. During the days of the trip and still that morning, a letter of St. Ireneus had impressed a great charge upon me. St. Ireneus had written that *"The Church is a sign raised up amongst the nations for the salvation of all"*. I had understood it in my own way, just as I had read in my own way the same reflection of the Second Vatican Council in the constitutions Lumen Gentium (48) and Gaudium et Spes (45): *"The Church is the universal sacrament of salvation... Christ, seated at the right hand of the Father, works in the world in order to guide men to the Church and with the Eucharist make them participants of it"*. I paused in my consideration especially upon the last part of Ireneus' definition: *"for the salvation of all"*. And I would see the flock of Christ enlarging itself and containing all men. Not exactly in a triumphant sense, but at least in a quantative and visible sense. Did not the Redeemer in fact die for all? Did not he want everybody to be saved and to come to the knowledge of the truth?

That encounter with my Muslim brothers put my interpretation into crisis. I would look at them, standing still along the dusty trail, and I had to admit that they didn't have any interest in my presence and in my message. And yet even they were called to salvation. And yet I was there for them.

At that moment a light struck me and the accent slided to the beginning of St. Ireneus' phrase, on the word: the Church is a SIGN!

Of course salvation has to be proclaimed to everybody and the Church in fact reaches every remote angle of the earth. But the touching of hearts and seeing men bow at the baptismal font is the merit and work of God himself. It is up to the Church to be a sign amongst men.

A word had never spoken so clearly to me: the Church has to be a sign of salvation for all! The efficacy no longer depends upon the Church: if the sign exists and it's really a sign, the Lord will think about making his children enter into the kingdom.

Given that, then, I was the only Christian of the area, the priviledge and the responsibility of being a sign fell upon me.

I did not continue that morning my exploration of the territory and of the inhabitants for whom I had come. I returned upon my footsteps. Next to my iron sheet shack another one arose as hurriedly I had dared to pompously call it a church. A heap of stones meant the altar, a little metal case became the tabernacle. And I found myself crouched at length in front of the Sacrament.

The strike formulated itself into a life program. The sign has to be absolutely genuine, otherwise it can mean ambiguous things and point to erroneous goals. Just as John Paul II wrote in Redemptoris Missio (90): *"The real missionary is the saint"*, and Joseph Allamano: *"First saints, then missionaries"*. The Church-sign is almost an earthly expression of God, and it immediately makes us look at all of humanity as a brotherhood!

A catechist soon arrived, whom the Bishop had sent me from far away. Then a little group of Sisters arrived. We all understood that we were the Church, that is disciples gathered around the divine Master.

We above all understood that the Church considered that rudimentary altar, which made Calvary present, as the 'peak and source' of all of its life. It was as if saying: 'He is the Redeemer and He is here. He is the missionary and He is here!'.

We got down to work in favour of the people: the school, the dispensary, the well arose... The poor were listened to and everybody felt at home in the mission's compound. Even a new sense of fraternity was beginning to be breathed in the distant villages. But the light came from the prayer shack, while waiting to have a beautiful church. Everybody entered in: the first catechumens, pagans, Muslims.

Everybody loved the silence and the peace which the place inspired. They probably did not know what the altar and especially the tabernacle meant, but they felt at ease and they would move around that place with great respect.

Recently, the Congregation for the Doctrine of the Faith wrote that *"Communion turns the faithful into members of the same body, the mystical body of Christ, a structured organic community, a people reunited into the unity of the Father, of the Son and of the Holy Spirit, moreover gifted with the means that permit its visual and social union"* (Communionis Notio).

The Christian community lives in invisible communion with God the Trinity and with the mystical body, and of visible communion that derives from it and embraces the whole span of life (Cfr. id.).

When Luther doubted the Eucharist, it seemed that the whole liturgical celebration reduced itself to remembering the paschal mystery lived out by Christ on Calvary and that, as a result, the tabernacles didn't have any meaning: the memory would cease with the celebration. The Council of Trent intervened accurately redefining the 'real presence'. From then until now we go on repeating that the incarnate Word is truly, really, corporally present in the eucharistic sacrament.

So, the eucharistic presence is understood as the uninterrupted sacrifice of Christ. It's therefore a dynamic and very vivid presence. It is the continued Mass. What takes place at the moment of consecration and at communion extends itself in time.

In order to remember it and to mean it, the recent documents of the Church on the eucharistic cult suggest to expose to the faithful on the altar, for functions of adoration, the host consecrated in the previous Mass and to let them see the continuation even in the same style of prayer and of the preparation of the altar.

The eucharistic cult is then fully justified and becomes a necessity. Everybody can understand its intimate dynamism: it's living out the Mass, it's remaining in communion. The time following the celebration makes the living Christ always interceding for us, exactly like during the moment of the consecration and of communion.

Adoration is placing oneself in this paschal state again and allowing oneself to be saved and transformed.

The church is "a sign raised up amongst the nations for the salvation of all" especially beginning from the Eucharist in its reality first as a sacrifice and then as a presence.

In the desert, from that altar, I saw a Christian community, that is a Church, born, it too a sign amongst the nations for the salvation of all. I noticed the fulfillment of the Word of God, as is read in Isaiah (19:19-26):

"On that day there will be an altar to Yahweh in the center of the land of Egypt and a sacred pillar to Yahweh at its border. It will be a sign and a remembrance of Yahweh Sabaoth when they are oppressed, and he will send a saviour to defend and deliver them.

Yahweh will reveal himself to the Egyptians. They will acknowledge him on that day and worship him with sacrifice and burnt offerings. [...] On that day there will be a highway from Egypt to Assyria. Assyrians will come to Egypt, and Egyptians to Assyria. Egyptians and Assyrians will worship together.

On that day, Israel will be a third party with Egypt and Assyria – a blessing on earth. And Yahweh will bless them saying, 'Blessed be Egypt my people, Assyria my creation, and Israel my heritage'".

THE CURE OF THE SUN

Eugene has been on the missionary frontier for some years now. On the eve of his priestly ordination, he gathered a group of friends in order to pray and to prepare for the great day.

That evening, I saw a happy man. He would not stop thanking the Lord for having called him and brought him to the priesthood. He would thank for the gift of a tranquil and joyous chastity, for the detachment from earthly goods and for the availability to any kind of obedience in any part of the world. He felt that he was modeled well, with harmony and completeness.

At a certain point he said to me: *"I think that all of these gifts are owed in a particular way to eucharistic adoration"*. He explained to me:

"When I entered into the missionary Institute at the age of 18, he who had accompanied me in discerning my vocation had advised me that, if I wanted to

turn out to be a holy priest, I had to decide to dedicate myself to an hour of personal prayer everyday. I took the advice with seriousness, but it cost me a lot. I didn't know how to pray and then carving out an hour everyday was a great enterprise with all of the communitarian commitments and the pressure of school. However the stakes were too great and I was faithful.

During novitiate, we had a course of spiritual exercises entirely based upon the Eucharist. Then I convinced myself of the goodness of the advice received and I even learned to pray much easier both when I didn't know how to pray and when it turned out to be a little easier for me, I always considered myself like a little plant in a flowerbed under the sun. It had been the sun that took care of it, of warming it up, of nourishing it and of enriching it with all of its vegetation. It had been Jesus in the Blessed Sacrament who prepared me in this way for the priesthood".

When Emmanuel, a seminarian of a vast diocese, learnt of Eugene's experience, he made it his own and he called it *"The cure of the sun"*. He too was about to begin his theological studies: he even decided to travel along the same road.

He does not live far away from the beach and he is familiar with the crowds of bathers who believe in the bathing cures. He too has been practicing it, the spiritual one I mean, for some years, and now he's happily reaching the goal of his dreams. He is a rather meticulous and active type. He is involved in all the sectors of communitarian and pastoral life, and he likes keeping the seminary in order. But he does not compromise on the cure of the sun. It's evident that he has drawn clear formative advantages. In his correspondence he never omits mentioning it.

In the letter *"Dominicae Coenae"*, John Paul II connected the Eucharist with the Second Vatican Council: *"The animation and the deepening of the eucharistic cult are proof of that authentic renewal which the Council has decided on as an objective and is its central point"*. A comment affirms that *"John Paul II has indicated in eucharistic adoration the real test of fidelity to the Second Vatican Council"* (Giulio Panzeri).

Every pastor of souls, every consecrated person, just like every lay person, especially if he is responsible for a family or for other people, has to know that in adoration he finds the meaning of his service and the first manner of exercising it.

St. Gregory the Great, commenting on the passage of Ezekiel *"I have placed you as a watchman over the house of Israel"* (Ezekiel 3:16), feels his own responsibility: *"What kind of a watchman am I who, instead of being on the mountain at work, still waver in the valley of weakness?"*. But he positively reflects:

"It is to be noted that when the Lord sends a person to preach, He calls him with the name of a watchman. The watchman in fact is always at an elevated place, in order to be able to notice from a distance anything that is about to happen. Whoever is placed as a watchman of the people must stay on high and live a blameless life". Being on high is a good way to indicate eucharistic prayer.

The stories of our first missionaries, who planted the Church in Africa with a lot of prayer, even at times waking up in the morning still on the altar step, have always edified me a lot. Brother Thomas had purposely built his carpentry shop at the back of the church's presbytery, so that his work would be a continuation of the Mass and so would be adoration. And sensational conversions of difficult people and of entire groups of pagans were told of, obtained in that way.

Even the Bible refers that when Moses went to the tent of gathering, without gathering the people, everybody would prostrate himself at the entrance of their tents, for the entire duration of their chief's prayer (Cfr. Exodus 33:8-11). And it even refers to Moses praying on the hill. All of us remember the victory of the people in battle due to its raised up hands (Cfr. Exodus 17:8-16).

When, in the desert mission, I read to my first catechumens the story of the liberation of the chosen people from slavery in Egypt, we listened to the narrative of the presence of God through the cloud that accompanied the fugitives. During the night the cloud was bright in order to ease the journey. During the day it mitigated the scorching rays of the sun (Cfr. Exodus 13:21-22). A catechumen, particularly attentive and intelligent, was conquered by the biblical narrative and came to tell me: *"Father, in our Borana language there is the explanation of the presence of God in front of his people. In Borana, God is called 'Waq', but even cloud is called 'waq'".* The same name!

One day I had asked him: *"Halkano, do the Borana pray?".*

He had answered back to me convincingly: *"The Borana pray continuously".* It did not appear to me that they had formal prayers. Their very idea of God, as I seemed to perceive it, was extremely vague. But that observation that God and cloud had a sole name made me understand it. The Borana have not formularies of prayer, as we have in the liturgy, but they have an uncertain concept of God, and yet their life is, just as for Abraham, a journeying in the presence of God (Cfr. Genesis 17:1). Just like whoever walks under the cloud.

Maybe he does not speak to the cloud, but he is covered by it: all of his moving is *"under the cloud"*.

It seemed to me a great thing coming from pagans. It seemed a splendid lesson to me just like a preparation in order to welcome the revelation, the Eucharist, real prayer! I even caught a glimpse of a very encouraging synthesis between prayer and life, between contemplation and action. Those catechumens, who did not have a preceding Christian community in which to reflect themselves, were so enthusiastic about the Gospel and they would live it out with edifying freshness as they would get to know it little by little. Now I understood it: they came from a kind of continuous prayer.

When Blessed Joseph Allamano said to his missionaries: *"I want you to be sacramentines"*, he knew very well that he was addressing himself to people immersed in the apostolate and in every kind of social activity. For him prayer served to multiply actions.

He even said that more is done in a quarter of an hour after having prayed than in two hours without prayer. That quarter of an hour enjoys divine fecundity and even gushes forth from an ordered mind and from energies put at full disposition. In any case, he says that one has to begin from prayer.

The altar is the source of the Church's life.

THE EUCHARISTIC FACE
OF MARY

During the war, a girl was deceived by a soldier from northern Europe with a promise of marriage. The war adventure ended and the invading army disappeared. The girl ended up with a very beautiful child, with two drops of the very blue sky as eyes. She was absolutely shocked and confused. Even the family felt ashamed and did not cooperate. The child ended up in a foundling hospital and was totally abandoned. The sisters loved him very much and so the atmosphere of the little orphan was serene. But only apparently.

The little child grew up and knew how to be in the company of others, but the intimate wound was acute. He would never talk about it. When he would see some relatives coming to visit his friends, he would suffer terribly about it inside. He had never seen his mother's face.

When he began to express himself he even began to boast about his mother. Even he had one he would say to his little friends, and one day she would have come to visit him and she would have brought gifts for everybody. His mother in fact was very beautiful, very rich and very generous.

At Christmas, the sisters prepared a nativity scene with big life-size statues: it occupied half of the hall. A curtain hid everything and the children's hearts beat strongly awaiting to see. They even rehearsed on the eve. The chaplain acted as the speaker and announced the characters: they were many but the attention was above all directed to the child and to his mother. He would describe them with a deep, moved and mysterious voice. In the evening the curtains would have been pulled away.

Later on everybody would have an afternoon nap. Except for a sister who would pray upon a big chair, at the end of the hall of the nativity scene. Angelo (this is what they called him), in the half-light, thinking that he had not been seen, arrived tiptoeing, placed himself near the curtain and began to talk to Jesus: *"I don't have a mother. You have one. I'm asking you for a great favour: lend me your mother, even only for a while, so that I can look at her as if she were mine and show her to my companions!"*.

He did not know that Jesus had already done it: the fourth Gospel narrates that while he was hanging on the cross, Jesus said to John: *"Here is your mother!"* (John 19:27). John was there as our representative. Jesus celebrated Mass on Calvary!

Mary took part in the lives of the first Christians. It was a very particular community and the presence of Jesus' mother constituted the pivot of unity and of everybody's fervor: *"All of these were assiduous and united in prayer, together with some women and with Mary, Jesus' mother, and with his brothers"* (Acts 1:14).

Their unity is described many times (Cfr. Acts 2:42-48; 4:32-35).

And it was during a special convocation that the Holy Spirit descended and transformed the disciples into apostles: *"When they finished their prayer, the place where they had gathered shook and all were full of the Holy Spirit and proclaimed the word of God with frankness"* (Acts 4:31).

Mary's role is to precisely bring Jesus to the world and the world to Jesus. Her presence seems to carry it out exactly at Mass.

✶ The penitential rite is the conversion of humanity that has experienced rebellion, but now enjoys the 'remission of sins'. She, Immaculate, tells us in a good way how God has thought about man and how He re-makes him through repentance, by giving him mercy.

✶ At the liturgy of the Word, Mary relives the listening of the day in which the angel Gabriel came to reveal to her God's plan. Her listening is perfectly expressed in her compliance: *"Here I am! Let your Word be done to me"* (Luke 1:38). And her teaching to her children is just as much clear, like it was at Cana: *"Do everything that he will tell you to do"* (John 2:5). The Word, in the Annunciation, came to live in her. At Mass, it comes to live in us.

✶ Mary is the closest to the Son of God and to her own who celebrates Easter on Calvary. *"She stood"* (John 19:25) near the cross and at the empty sepulchre. She describes the participation which the Church asks of us, very concerned *"that the faithful should not assist as strangers or mute spectators at this mystery of faith, but that, by understanding it by means of the rites and of the prayers, participate consciously, fully and actively in the sacred action"* (Sacrosanctum Concilium 48). Mary's attitude expresses the welcoming of the salvation plan and the sharing of the gift itself. Mary is redeemed and collaborates in redemption and we are taught to participate in the same way.

* And just like the Mass is Jesus' thanksgiving song for the divine plan of salvation, so Mary teaches us to consider with infinite and unceasing gratitude that the Lord has looked upon humanity's lowliness and has worked great things.
* Mass then projects the participants towards mission and even this is strongly typical of Mary. The Jesus whom she has conceived was to be born for the whole world. She showed it by taking him to Ain Karim, at Bethlehem, in Egypt, to Nazareth, to all the villages and to all the cities, right throughout the territory of his homeland.

The catechumens of the desert felt an attraction towards Mary much more beyond what catechesis taught them. It's evident that in Jesus' mother resides a special fascination which attracts people. The catechumenal instruction obeys the law of essentiality: the Word has to be proclaimed and this is the first of all devotions. Scripture would be read slowly and it is known that a rather sober mention is reserved for Our Lady. And yet the catechumens didn't miss one word of the biblical references to Mary:

* A saviour has been promised, who will be born of a woman (Cfr. Galatians 4:4).

* He will be like the sun which is preceded by the dawn (Cfr. Genesis 3:15).
* He will be the son of a very special person, a virgin (Cfr. Isaiah 7:14).
* An angel will announce it and will reveal a divine plan (Cfr. Luke 1:26-38).
* At Christmas he will appear in his mother's arms (Cfr. Luke 2:7).
* He will grow in motherly company (Cfr. Luke 2:39-52).
* Even during His preaching, Mary will be with him, with discretion and an active presence (Cfr. Luke 8:19).
* Right until the cross (Cfr. John 19:25ff) and then in the cenacle of Pentecost (Cfr. Acts 1:14) she will always be there.

When, during our catechesis, the Gospel brought her as a protagonist at Nazareth and at Bethlehem, a little niche was prepared with a little statue in the mud wall of every hut. Mary had entered into their homes, become a part of their families, and with her they would become Christians.

One had invented a formula that guided many moments of his life: *"Kwa ajili ya Maria"* (= for the sake of Mary!). He would repeat it during beautiful times as a thanksgiving, in difficult times as a recourse for some help, in ordinary times in order to declare how he wanted to act. One day he went to help a neighbour of his with some manual work. That friend of his was so poor that he felt embarassed for not being able to reward him. He explained to him: *"I haven't come for a reward. I came kwa ajili ya Maria"*.

Another day, he repeated to me that a Muslim had attacked him, showing a bit of contempt towards the catechumens. He had said to him: *"You Christians aren't any better than the others. You do what everybody else does"*. He answered him: *"It's true. Many times I don't act correctly. But when I open the door of my hut, I find Mary's statue on the front wall. I stop in front of her and her goodness immediately purifies me"*.

Jesus has truly made us participants in everything that he has, including his mother!

Even Douglas Hyde, a famous English journalist, spoke about his own conversion. Mary was there at the beginning of his new life. He wrote: *"One day I entered a Catholic Church and I sat at the back. Only in order to rest; it was the only tranquil place in the vicinity. After a while I saw a young girl enter in. She was maybe about 18 years old. She didn't dress well and was manifestly perturbed. She stopped for an instant in front of the altar, then she went on to kneel in front of an image of Mary. She let a few coins drop in a little box, lit up a candle and prayed for a long while. When she left and passed next to me, she had a face full of peace. I did exactly the same because I felt very agitated inside. I went to the altar, turned to the left, knelt down in front of the image, let a few coins drop and lit up a candle. The candle was almost consumed and I still hadn't formulated a prayer: I didn't know any at all. I finally remembered something read in Chesterton and in Belloc and said: Lady, be good to me! I left with so much peace. A few days later, exactly on the 17th of January, 1948, I began preparation for baptism. My wife and my two children were with me also".*

Christian life is really an *"experience of configuration to Christ, according to the example of and with the help of Mary"* (Lumen Gentium 62).

A DESIRE FOR
THE PRIESTHOOD

Vocation promotion work should pour forth spontaneously from the Mass.

Thirty years ago, MOYALE, the last mission born in the desert of Marsabit, in northern Kenya, did not count one single Christian. A promising array of catechumens and of sympathizers dawned like a springtime, with the arrival of the Gospel. The freshness of the communities of the Acts of the Apostles could be breathed.

Many boys and youth saw school for the first time and there was great enthusiasm for books, but even more still for the new Life.

Attentive care was reserved for a little group of these so that with time they would become 'leaders' of their people.

Halkano Boru showed a lot of diligence. At the age of 16 he dedicated himself with commitment to school. His whole person was well-disposed:

laborious, serene, open. Every Word of the Lord listened to became life for him. In the sharing, he would show a mature vision of the problems. The rearing of camels was his main interest; drought constantly afflicted the desert; tribal conflicts and raids tore social relationships apart; the needy did not have prospects due to the absence of charitable structures. Halkano's observations often recognized in the Gospel the source of hopes and of solutions.

For two years he had been attending the cate-chumenate with fidelity. He was half way towards the end: the curriculum foresaw four years of pre-paration for baptism.

One day, during one of the regular conver-sations, he looked at me smilingly as if he had something special to tell me. I generally spoke very little, trying to listen with love. Finally he conti-nued:

"Father, yesterday I was observing you while you were at the altar. You touched the things and read the Word of God to the people. Everybody listened with great interest. A very vivid desire grew in my heart and I prayed like this: How I would like, Jesus, to be even next to the father one day, I too touching the things like he does and I too reading the Word of God to the people!".

I stopped him: *"You see, Halkano, you are still all pagans here. How can you talk about priesthood?".*

He looked at me with a disarming smile: *"But, Father, you will soon baptize us!"*.

I continued: *"Here all of the adults are married. Only I am not married for Jesus"*.

He rebutted: *"We didn't know. But I want to be like you"*.

Halkano never became a priest on this earth. Snatched from the desert for another destination, I kept contact with him and the seminary project was progressing. That young man would have been the first seminarian of the desert. He was ready to reach Nairobi.

There was no public transport then and the police would concede a lift to whoever really had to face the crossing. A real human cluster crammed up onto the Land Rover that time, which, in the heart of the desert, at full speed slid on stony ground. Some died, including Halkano.

During a trip to Kenya, I traveled around the area. Some nomads who were grazing their meager flock indicated the place of the accident to me. It was not possible to find out details of how things had gone and what ever happened to the corpses. I was only able to kneel down amongst the volcanic rocks and I would have loved to pause there at length.

When a Church is born Providence also wants to think about pastors that are actually from that community. St. Paul founded churches, but before leaving in his itinerary, he would supply the new foundations with adequate leaders and, if possible, from the same place.

Even Blessed Allamano encouraged his first missionaries to look after primary evangelization but soon was thinking about the possibility of a seminary. Wasn't it Blessed Daniel Comboni's motto: *"Saving Africa with Africa?"* And did not Paul VI do the same, wishing during the canonization ceremony of the Ugandan Martyrs that *"May Africa be evangelized by Africans?"*.

MISSION, after the Second Vatican Council, charges itself ever more with a new force that comes from St. Teresa of the Child Jesus, 'Doctor of the Church'.

Mission had been the natural component of her spiritual life, to the point that the Church saw her as the patroness of missions! For everybody it is the natural component of spiritual life. The Second Vatican Council which recognizes every baptized person as a missionary knows it very well. From then on we're learning to think of ourselves and to recognize ourselves as such. First, mission had a more directly geographical connotation and indicated non evangelized territories. Teresa Martin perceived in the Holy Spirit the universality of the Word and of the Faith. A vocation to depart grew in her.

Her deepest aspiration, from the cell of the cloister, made her consider herself 'consecrated, spouse and mother': entirely belonging to God and entirely belonging to humanity! Ready even to depart for a foundation in a non-Christian territory, she decided that her last sufferings should be her missionary journey covering the whole expanse of geography and of history! A few weeks before dying, she wrote to her brother, Fr. Roulland, a missionary in China: *"When you receive this letter I will have surely left the earth! Rest assured that your little sister will keep her promises and her soul, freed from her mortal body, will fly happily towards the distant regions evangelized by you"*. Death seems to still more definitely consecrate our missionary vocation.

'CONTEMPLATION AND MISSION' are certainly words that describe Teresa but, even with us, mission is, first of all, in the heart. From there it generates inner life and the giving of oneself without limits.

I carry within myself a time lived in the desert, during the primary evangelization which is truly 'primary'. There was not even a Christian because colonization policy had sealed up a vast desert territory as 'no man's land': those brethren had never seen a school, a hospital and a church. From them I learned how the Gospel is for the little ones and for the poor and how one opens oneself up to it. The thirst of the land expresses well the thirst for the Word. And it's wonderful how the freshness of whoever welcomes the Gospel for the first time communicates itself to the missionaries and wakens them up again to the truth proclaimed.

Pronouncing the name of Jesus for the first time in those places gives rise to the mist vivid wonder: they recognize that He is the real missionary of humanity and that his gift is the sharing of God's life to men. Everything moves around Him who is omnipresent, although invisible. The people come, rejoice and begin to stop in prayer around this Invisible One. They then begin to recognize themselves as the family of God. This is such a new fact that it provokes new ways of getting acquainted amongst brothers. The sharing of this Christian love even develops new things, which seem to come first but instead are a derivation of it: schools, dispensaries and social life become ways of expressing this new life and have the taste of it. The nomads of the desert have even learnt to appreciate some agricultural products that during the rainy season can grow and strengthen their health. But the Word of God has constituted the sun of a new era, fertile with new life and with a further mission.

Two boys, Duba and Bonaya, had just begun the catechumenate. According to me they were very promising, so great was their commitment and their fidelity. And yet after a few weeks they disappeared. I felt a vivid regret about it, but there was no reason to be too surprised about it. The nomads come and go with ease and at times move hundreds of kilometers away. After a long month, my friends showed up again. They were exhausted and in a bad state, but full of joy. To my anxious questions, they answered: *"One day you read from the book that Jesus wants us to be born a second time. He came for this reason. We liked it so much and we decided to be reborn. But we thought about all of the people of our tribe who live far away in the desert did not know about it and no longer had to remain ignorant about it. So we went to tell everybody in the villages about it"*. They had traveled almost ninety kilometers without means and without a knapsack! But the Word gives rise to apostles, catechists and candidates to the priesthood.

In our times, the word MISSION is used very often and it seems that it has to embrace every expression of life. And it is like this. This how the Second Vatican Council and all the documents of the Church talks about it today. Only that it has to be a word which really expresses its contents. MISSION expresses God's plan to make men participants in his life and therefore tells of his passionate love for humanity. In order to carry this design out there has been the incarnation and Calvary. God himself is, therefore, the first missionary and everyone must let Him enter into his life. MISSION has an 'inner' dimension and also a 'boundless' dimension, which does not allow even one of these *"little ones"* (Matthew 25:40) to ignore this divine and fabulous Story.

A young man who perceives within himself a missionary vocation is absorbed by it and can discover in the intimacy of his heart that God has chosen him *"in order to go and bear fruit"*. Vocation is not a human choice. Jesus said it so clearly: *"I have chosen you!"*. Vocational pastoral work, then, does not give rise to vocations, but recognizes them in the depths of the individuals called from eternity.

Looking after vocations is above all *"praying the Lord of the harvest"* (Matthew 9:38), and as pedagogy is leading the youth to Christ, like Andrew did when he led his brother to Jesus, who loved him and called him (Cfr. John 1:42).

"Of course, if there are good sheep, there will also be good shepherds, because from good sheep good shepherds are formed. All good shepherds identify themselves with their own sheep, whom they know and who know them. In them who graze is Christ who grazes" (St. Augustine, Discourse 46, On shepherds).

Mass as the fulcrum of divine love and communion, as the point of maximum divine intimacy, constitutes the most fascinating vocational moment. Halkano felt himself called at Mass!

MISSIONARY ANIMATION

My mother hadn't studied a lot. She was a little girl during the First World War and all of her big brothers were at the front. There were things to do at home: the little children had to be looked after, provide for the running of the home and helping out in the fields. One would go to school in one's spare time. But her vivid intelligence allowed her to increase her culture a lot by reading and listening in all possible circumstances.

When I was in the desert, I would receive many letters of hers and with wonder I would see that exercise would make her progress quickly. She even improved her calligraphy. But her thoughts were those that would express the wisdom of classical mothers. I would hear once again the wisdom of Mother Mary Anne Cafasso-Allamano, of Mother Margaret Bosco, and of many women who in the hard and laborious environment, in the presence of

God, knew how to understand life and suggest wise advice.

A letter of hers, written on paper with little squares, ripped from a notebook, is still in my memory which I don't dare destroy. It says: *"From my married children, I receive many consolations and even tribulations. From my missionary children, I only receive consolations"*.

Once, during a brief holiday, while I was seated in the study room on the floor above, I heard her chatter in the street with our next door neighbour who lived in front of us. They were talking to each other about the difficulties of life with regard to health, the family and a thousand other ordinary things. The other woman did not attend the Church and her tone was often bitter. My mother listened to her at length and then said to her: *"You know, I too have all of these disappointments; but I've found a solution: the Mass"*. And she told her how everyday she found strength and serenity by going to deposit her baggage at the altar. She would always return from it with the energy that only communion can give. And she concluded: *"Mass is everything for me!"*.

My mother uttered the solemn words of the Second Vatican Council *"Culmen et Fons"*: *"Mass is everything for me!"*.

And at a certain point she proposed to her: *"Why don't you come as well. If you like, tomorrow morning I'll ring your doorbell and we'll go together"*.

And it came about exactly like that: every morning my mother would leave early, would wait for her friend to come down and together would head off to church.

Today missionary animation is an important chapter of all of the local churches and requires the full time dedication of many members of missionary Institutes, which obedience holds back in their native countries.

Offices in every diocese and in every missionary house have been organized. The initiatives are many and intelligent and missionary animation groups have arisen everywhere. It actually seems that the far distant world has arrived at home and nobody ignores the situations of the various continents. Solidarity is begged, is welcomed, is solicited. Many young people and many adults go to see how things are elsewhere. Many give time and energy and feel like missionaries at the frontline.

The departure point for all of this movement is the altar.

Missionary animation wants in fact God's passionate love for humanity lived and be lived and this love has its fulcrum in Calvary, where *"He loved right until the end"* (John 13:1).

One becomes a missionary in the first place by living out this sacrifice of salvation which we have in the Eucharist.

Around the altar by becoming one with Christ, the Church becomes aware of its being missionary and, by letting itself be evangelized it becomes an evangelizer.

Every act of generosity and any good worked on earth always contains a participation in God's love, because *"Only God is good!"* (Matthew 19:17). Jesus said that anything done to any neighbour is done unto Him (Cfr. Matthew 25:40). Everything that goes under the title of social progress and of human promotion arises from the charity and from the action of the Holy Spirit, even if at times it has an exclusive horizontal appearance.

Education for mission, however, has to lead to the source and to full collaboration in the mystery of salvation.

Everything comes about at Mass.

For this reason the heart of missionary animation and of all charity has to be the Eucharist.

Father Charles de Foucauld has been indicated by Paul VI, in the encyclical *'Populorum Progressio'*, as a *"model for every missionary"*. A model, even, for missionary animation, both at home and on the 'ad gentes' frontier.

His followers expressed in the following way his thoughts comparing their vocation in three points: *"imitating Our Lord Jesus in his hidden life of Nazareth"*, *"practising perpetual adoration of the Blessed Sacrament"* and *"living in mission territories"*. The holy Host exposed day and night makes their lives similar to that of Mary's and of Joseph's, given that, just like them, they have Our Lord Jesus under their eyes at any hour. By taking their altar and their tabernacle to the midst of non-christian peoples they silently sanctify these peoples, just like Jesus of Nazareth sanctified the world for thirty years in silence.

When Fr. De Foucauld enthroned the first tabernacle in the lands of the Tuareg, beneath the tent, he prayed like this:

"Jesus, thank you for this first tabernacle. That it be the prelude of many others and the proclamation of the salvation of so many souls! Irradiate from the depth of this tabernacle upon the people who surround you without knowing you. Enlighten, guide, save these souls that you love. Convert and sanctify the Tuareg, Morocco, the Sahara, the pagans, all men! Send saints and numerous evangelical workers amongst the Tuareg, in the Sahara, in Morocco, wherever there is need.

And convert me".

SIGN OF UNITY,
BOND OF CHARITY

The Mass of that Monday morning was lived out like a real missionary mandate for the young sisters of Mother Teresa of Calcutta who the day before had made their religious profession. They were now ready for any charity to which they would be appointed. And it was exactly after Mass that the Mother would have announced the various destinations. A climate of evident generosity blew but a sense of trepidation was also natural.

Mother Teresa said to one: *"You'll go to the hospital for the dying, up there"*, and she readily moved, showing a great smile. The Mother cried out to her from behind: *"I suppose you know well with what attitude to get there"*. The young girl stopped, came back and said: *"I think I know, but tell me once again, please"*. And the Mother: *"Did you see with what love the priest this morning touched Jesus on the altar. Go and do the same"*. The young girl left with ebullience. In the late morning she arrived running into Mother Teresa's office: *"Mother, Mother, I touched Jesus for three hours!. – And how?. – They brought a man found on the pebbly shore of the river to the hospital for the dying. He was more dead than alive, all wounds, mud and insects. It took three hours in order to clean him, treat him, dress him up once again. Now he's there, without any hope of surviving, but clean and serene. I knew I was touching Jesus' Body!"*.

It tastes so much like the parable of the good Samaritan; but it makes one reflect upon the comparison: body of Christ = brother! The source is the Mass: *"a sign of unity, a bond of charity"* (Sacrosanctum Concilium 47).

In fact, St. Augustine widely taught that the body of Christ is the *"Entire Christ"*: Jesus, that is, embraces in himself his community of origin and the community that he has assumed with the incarnation. Seeing Him is seeing the Trinity, and also the whole of humanity. And touching any brother or sister is touching Him (Cfr. Matthew 25:40).

Communion, as a consequence, establishes a deep unity with everybody and generates more genuine brotherly love. The Church, built by the Eucharist, is 'extroverted', the Pope said commenting upon the diocesan mission of Rome and blessing two thousand 'missionary' citizens.

Generosity is born of true eucharistic communion.

During a day of missionary spirituality for youth, the Mass has to constitute the height of the meeting. The atmosphere was saturated with joy and that young crowd promised itself once again to give a very high meaning to life. In order to give effect their love to Jesus, who grasped their hearts so revealingly, a small project in favour of young lepers in a lost Ethiopian locality had been proposed to them. The animators had specified: *"It's a sign to offer to Jesus. Anything can be it, even a written testimony"*. In the little basket, filled with bank notes and with little letters, a note said: *"Jesus, I understand what you've done for me. I too give you everything: I give you myself"*. It could have alluded to the consecration of one's life, but, more importantly, it declared that the Mass had conquered him completely and had turned his life into a gift.

He, too, had entered into the Mass as a disciple and had left as an apostle.

Elizabeth Catez had *"taken off"*. She was not a Carmelite Sister yet and she was only 16 years old. She was a very spiritually mature young girl, but she was also committed to all of the expressions of social life. At Dijon, cultural conferences for the population were frequently held. At times there were conferences with a religious topic and once the speaker had to deal with the Trinity. The speaker was Fr. Vallée, a brilliant and famous Dominican. He said that the Trinity lives in the baptized person. They had told Elizabeth for years that her name actually meant the same thing. Fr. Vallée's conversation found her prepared and literally conquered her. After the conference she wanted to meet the priest. That talk seemed essential and infinitely beautiful to her and she did not want to undervalue it. The priest confirmed to her: *"Yes, God the Father lives in you, God the Son lives in you, God the Holy Spirit lives in you!"*.

Elizabeth will write with regard to that moment: *"The Word struck me"*. She never forgot it.

Even Fr. Vallée, years later, described the encounter: *"I had noticed that Elizabeth had 'taken off'"*.

Elizabeth didn't go very far, physically. She instead reached the most sublime peak of holiness.

At Mass, the Trinitarian inhabitation is given to us today. It is exactly what Jesus affirms: *"Whoever eats my flesh and drinks my blood lives in me and I live in him"* (John 6:56). The Second Vatican Council notes: it is baptism brought to fullness now.

And after Mass one departs: one departs in order to love everybody, in order to give everything!

111

Luigi Bracco founded the *"Mass for the poor"* in the diocese of Fossano. He was a lawyer but the Gospel was his real profession. He had made the radical choice of working only for what allowed him to live and to dedicate the rest of his time to prayer and to the poor. Every Sunday he would gather all of the poor of the city and would take them for Mass to shrines, to religious centers in the vicinities, with lunch paid for. He would prepare these Masses with care and the celebrant had to give a real welcoming to the guests. When it was possible the Bishop would accompany them. The Mass deserved these attentions but even the poor deserved them. Almost at the same level.

THANKING

The lay members of the Consolata Missionary Institute have the right to ask a priestly confrère to celebrate a Mass every month for their intentions.

Brother Joseph Michieletto had been a faithful 'eucharistic missionary' for 64 years, almost entirely spent in Africa. He died recently at the age of 86.

He lived the last night of his life in a particular fervor and felt that even for him *"everything had been consumed"*.

That morning he spoke with commotion to the nursing father who looked after him and made up his bed. He told him, after having embraced him: *"Please, I ask you to celebrate the Mass today for me, as I have asked you monthly. But you have to celebrate the thanksgiving Mass. The Lord has filled my life with attention and with gifts, I have so much to be thankful for to so many people who have helped me, for my missionary vocation, for infinite graces. Father, I only have to give thanks and I'll depart content".*

It seemed that he did not have to ask for forgiveness. No fear, no regret seemed to perturb him. It was evident that God's peace inundated him and all he wanted to do was to give thanks.

He died on that very same day and the father celebrated Mass for him: the Mass of thanksgiving. He had to carry out the brother's wish.

Brother Joseph did just as Jesus did. Even Jesus offered his life giving thanks.

"When the hour came for the paschal supper, Jesus took the chalice, thanked God... Then took the bread, said the prayer of thanksgiving" (Luke 22:14-20).

Jesus seals the new and eternal covenant, he carries out the Historia Salutis, carries out the Father's design and gives thanks. He carries out EUCHARIST (= thanksgiving). He gives thanks for the divine plan centered in the paschal mystery. He gives thanks for his DEATH and for his RESURRECTION.

It means that thanksgiving pervades the life of God and the life of the universe.

The Talmud makes an unceasing acknowledgement of it: "Blessed are you, Lord:

✶ for this piece of bread (because you provide),
✶ for this glass of wine,

114

* for the sandals, a wheat field, a friend,
* for a bad piece of news (because you lead everything to good),
* for a bad thing (because you know how to judge)… ".

We especially give thanks by participating in the Eucharist and receiving the Body of Christ. In this moment there aren't adequate words: the thanksgiving consists in the awareness and in allowing that the mystery inundates us and fulfills itself. One of the definitions of communion, as a background, can help us:

* *"We become what we receive"* (St. Leo the Great),
* *"Whoever eats… lives in me, I in him"* (John 6:56),
* *"Communion is the fusion of existences"* (Card. J. Ratzinger).

Spiritual communion, just like the visit to the Blessed Sacrament and adoration, revive sacramental communion.

One has to above all make one's entire life a thanksgiving. Just like Mary made her life a *Magnificat*. Conformed to Christ, we are new creatures.

Thanksgiving is in God's very nature. God is Trinity, which means Love, Gift. Trinitarian love is the circulation of the gift. The Father makes a total gift of himself in the Son. The Son gives back all of himself to the Father. *"And this is so true, the recipro-cal gift which one is for the other, is 'given' so much, and definitely given, that the reciprocity of the gift does not return neither to the Father nor to the Son, but, exactly because the gift is total, it is not the Father and it is not the Son; it is the Holy Spirit 'who procedes from the Father and from the Son'. Here is the Third of the Trinity, which is not a number but the fulfill-ment of the perfect circulation of Love. Three because not one; not two; three as love without repentance, without reserve, without interest"* (G. Casoli, *Se dico grazie*).

"Nothing is more urgent than the thanksgiving" (St. Ambrose). But we often do not think about it, like egoistic children, to whom everything is owed. *"What does ingratitude procede from? From love of oneself. Man doesn't see himself 'not being'. If he were to see, he would know that he has received being and every grace from God, because only God is He who is"* (St. Catherine of Siena, Letter 337). We have to re-educate ourselves to gratitude, because everything that we are and that we have, we have received.

Even earthly goods: *"If we do not attribute to God the goods that we enjoy in this world how can we expect from Him the goods promised in the life to come?"* (St. Seraphim of Sarov).

Especially the gift of life: *"Friends are thanked who give us a box of cigars or a pair of slippers for our birthday. Can I not thank Someone who for my first birthday has given me the gift of life?"* (G. Chesterton, Orthodoxy).

The greatest gift is that of faith, such a precious gift that we logically want everybody to be able to enjoy it and for this reason the Church is missionary. *'Fidei donum!'*.

Whoever participates at Mass also participates in Jesus' dialogue with the Father: *"Jesus was full of joy by the work of the Holy Spirit and said: I thank you, Father, Lord of heaven and earth. I thank you!"* (Luke 10:21).

There is a moment in the Lord's life, that due to its intensity places itself as a transition between the Christ in the flesh and the Christ mystically prolonged in time: this key moment is the Last Supper. It is certainly for Jesus a culminating point, awaited and longed for at length by him, the supreme and final hour of his earthly existence.

The Supper holds an analogous importance for the life of the Church: a threshold between the physical Christ and the Christ mystically actualized in time, it is the seal of love of the former and the source of life of the latter.

"Do this in memory of me": with these words Jesus entrusts to the Apostles the mandate to celebrate in history the memorial of his Easter. The Eucharist is the event that carries out the Church's evangelizing mission in the highest degree: celebrating the memorial of the Lord,

the Church makes herself available to the action of the Spirit, which makes the event of salvation, the object of the Good News, present in the diversity of times and places. The Last Supper presents to us in such a dense and lively manner the passage from the Servant's Word to servants of the Word, from the evangelizing Christ to evangelizing Church.

The characteristics conferred by Jesus to his Church's evangelizing mission turn out to be in such a manner clearly singled out: announcing the Gospel right until the extreme ends of the earth means, in the light of the Lord's Eucharist, introducing Christ again in the variety of places and times, in the power of the Spirit, in ecclesial communion, at the world's service and under the sign of the cross, preparing the promised glory of the Kingdom.

Mons. Bruno Forte